# just ainsley harriott
# five
## ingredients

# just

## ainsley harriott

# five

## ingredients

### Over 120 fast, fuss-free recipes

Published in 2009 by BBC Books, an imprint of Ebury Publishing.
A Random House Group Company

The Random House Group Limited Reg. No. 954009

Addresses for companies within the Random House Group can be found
at **www.randomhouse.co.uk**

A CIP catalogue record for this book is available from the British Library.

ISBN 978 0 56 353924 7

The Random House Group Limited supports The Forest Stewardship Council
(FSC), the leading international forest certification organization. All our titles
that are printed on Greenpeace approved FSC certified paper carry the FSC logo.
Our paper procurement policy can be found at www.rbooks.co.uk/environment

Commissioning editor: Muna Reyal
Project editor: Caroline McArthur
Copy-editor: Stephanie Evans
Designer: Smith & Gilmour
Food stylist: SPK
Prop stylist: Wei Tang
Production: David Brimble

All photography © Dan Jones except pp 10, 32, 56, 74 and 142 © Colin Bell

Colour origination, printing and binding by Butler Tanner & Dennis Ltd

10 9 8 7 6 5 4 3

**Mixed Sources**
Product group from well-managed
forests and other controlled sources
www.fsc.org  Cert no. SGS-COC-005091
© 1996 Forest Stewardship Council
FSC

# Contents

# Introduction

Cooking at home for family and friends is all about unpretentious meals and good ingredients. I've always enjoyed creating quick and simple recipes that are delicious to eat without compromising on flavour, but I've become increasingly aware of another element – the length of the ingredients list. I think we chefs focus so much on creating depth and flavour that we sometimes forget how much shopping and preparation we're asking our readers to do – how many times have you looked at a recipe but felt put off by the number of ingredients?

In this book you don't have to worry about what can be a daunting and overwhelming challenge, especially for the less experienced cook. Shorter shopping lists and reduced preparation times can be really useful for modern-day lifestyles, and even more so if you're on a budget.

I set myself a limit of just five ingredients plus salt, pepper and oil, to reflect this new style of modern cooking. And after creating 120 recipes for this book, I have to say I was genuinely excited and sometimes surprised at how delicious these dishes tasted. Cooking with only a few items can be very liberating as you can really taste each individual flavour. Nothing is hidden – in this case less is definitely more! Who would have thought you could make a succulent Thai red beef curry with just five ingredients? Well you can if you focus on the key ingredient combination that will maximize the flavour.

There are lots of fabulous side dishes and scrummy hot and cold desserts, like chocolate parfait terrine with fresh raspberries, baked pears with pecan nuts and golden syrup, or if you fancy keeping it fresh and simple, try pineapple carpaccio with chilli, mint and passion fruit syrup. For those of you who like to bake, try my Rustic walnut and raisin bread, traditional Irish soda bread or melt-in-the-mouth Lemon shortbread triangles.

This kind of cooking is also perfect for vegetarians because what better way is there to bring out the taste of the freshest, best-quality vegetables than by marrying them with a few choice ingredients – Baked field mushrooms going nuts with Cashel Blue, for example?

A short list of ingredients means that all of these recipes are very simple to prepare. Most will also take very little time to cook, but to maximise flavour, I have included a few recipes that do require some marinating time, or that take a little longer in the oven. But if you plan for this and check the recipe for timings beforehand, it will require no more effort from you.

Another tip is to have a good selection of store cupboard foods, so you'll always be able to knock up a tasty meal with hardly any effort. Remember you need just five ingredients to make a meal. So stock up on cans or jars of tomatoes, tinned or dried pulses, peppers or artichokes in olive oil, coconut milk, risotto or easy cook rice, a variety of pasta shapes, stock cubes or liquid stock, good-quality salt and pepper, sunflower oil and virgin olive oil.

I've also based each chapter around key ingredients depending on what you're likely to have in your fridge or store cupboard or what's available at your local supermarket. Each chapter has five recipes for one key ingredient. So if you fancy chicken tonight, have a look at the two chicken chapters. There are two chapters on pasta that are perfect for weeknight suppers, another that focuses on eggs and cheese, and one on mushrooms – I think mushrooms are hugely underrated.

I have divided the recipes into courses and groups – starters and light meals, pastas, pulses and grains, vegetarian dishes, meat and poultry, fish and seafood, side dishes, puddings and baking – but my recipes are really flexible, so although there is a starters and light meals section, there isn't one for main courses. Some recipes are obviously main courses, starters or puddings, but please do feel free to double the starters or light meal recipes to make a main meal, or reduce the quantities of a main meal to cook a light lunch. If you are vegetarian do also check out the recipes in starters and light meals and pastas, pulses and grains.

I hope you enjoy making these recipes as much as I enjoyed creating them.

*Ainsley Harriott*

# Starters and light meals

With five good ingredients, you can easily create a delicious starter or snack that's bursting with flavour. These recipes are perfect for a quick bite and, if you are entertaining, will really help take the pressure off. If you are planning a party, why not cook a selection of these small dishes.

# Tapas and small bites

# Manchego cheese fritters

These fritters need to be eaten not long after they are out of the pan.

❶ 3 tablespoons plain flour
❷ 350g (12oz) Manchego (or goats' cheese, mozzarella or Gruyère)
❸ 1 egg
❹ 75g (3oz) breadcrumbs, preferably from a day-old sourdough or ciabatta loaf
❺ 1 tablespoon chopped fresh flat-leaf parsley
& salt and freshly ground black pepper; sunflower oil, for frying

**serves 4–6 as a starter or for tapas**

**step one** Heat 5cm (2 inches) of the oil in a heavy-based frying pan. Meanwhile, place the flour on a plate and season generously. Cut the Manchego into 2cm (¾ inch) cubes and toss in the seasoned flour.

**step two** Beat the egg and seasoning in a bowl and mix the breadcrumbs and parsley in a separate shallow dish. Dip the floured cheese cubes into the beaten egg and then roll in the breadcrumbs. Lower them into the heated oil (you may need to do this in batches) and cook for 1–2 minutes until golden brown. Remove with a slotted spoon and drain on kitchen paper. Spear with cocktail sticks and arrange on a plate. Serve immediately.

# Creamy cheesy grilled smoked haddock

These smokies would also be great in a large dish for supper with a bowl of salad and plenty of ciabatta to mop up all those delicious juices.

❶ 450g (1lb) natural smoked haddock, skinned and boned
❷ 225g (8oz) cherry tomatoes, halved
❸ 4 spring onions, trimmed and finely chopped
❹ 250ml (9fl oz) carton crème fraîche
❺ 100g (4oz) Cheddar cheese, grated
& sea salt and freshly ground white pepper; 1 tablespoon sunflower oil

**serves 4 as a starter, or double the quantities for a main course**

**step one** Preheat the grill. Cut the haddock into four even-sized portions. Heat a frying pan and add the sunflower oil. Place the smoked haddock in the pan, presentation-side up, and cook for 2–3 minutes, then turn over and cook for another 1–2 minutes until cooked through and just tender; this will depend on the thickness of the fillets.

**step two** Add the cherry tomatoes and spring onions to the pan, tossing until lightly coated in the oil. Add the crème fraîche and season to taste. Cook and gently stir until the crème fraîche has bubbled up to form a sauce. Using a fish slice, transfer the haddock portions into individual ovenproof dishes and then spoon the cherry tomato and spring onion mixture on top. Scatter over the Cheddar and flash under the hot grill for 2–3 minutes until the Cheddar is bubbling and golden. Place the hot dishes on plates to serve.

# Asparagus with creamed mascarpone, cracked black pepper and Parmesan

This is a great dish to make when asparagus are in season and is a perfect starter for a dinner party as it can be made well in advance. I like to crack my own black pepper in a pestle and mortar as I find the flavour is always so much better, but of course you can buy it ready prepared from the supermarket.

1. 20 asparagus spears, trimmed
2. 250g (9oz) tub mascarpone
3. 50g (2oz) freshly grated Parmesan
4. 1 ciabatta loaf, sliced on the diagonal
&. sea salt and freshly cracked black pepper

**serves 4 as a starter**

**step one** Preheat the grill. Cook the asparagus in a pan of boiling salted water for 1 minute, then remove with a slotted spoon and quickly refresh in a bowl of iced water. Drain well on kitchen paper.

**step two** Place the mascarpone in a bowl and beat in two-thirds of the Parmesan, then season generously with the cracked black pepper.

**step three** Divide the asparagus spears among four small ovenproof dishes and spread the mascarpone mixture on top. Sprinkle over the remaining Parmesan.

**step four** Arrange the dishes on the grill rack and flash under the grill for 3–4 minutes until the mascarpone mixture is bubbling and lightly golden.

**step five** Transfer the hot dishes onto plates and add some slices of bread to each one before serving.

# Hot-smoked salmon and pink grapefruit salad with red pepper dressing

Hot-smoked salmon has a delicate smoky flavour and flaky texture.

1. 2 pink grapefruits
2. 100g (4oz) wild rocket
3. 225g (8oz) hot-smoked salmon
4. 1 roasted red pepper, drained (from a jar or can)
5. 2 teaspoons white wine vinegar
&. sea salt and freshly ground black pepper; 6 tablespoons extra-virgin olive oil

**serves 4 as a starter**

**step one** Peel and segment the grapefruits, discarding all the pith. Scatter the rocket on plates, arrange the grapefruit and roughly flake the hot-smoked salmon on top.

**step two** Place the red pepper in a mini food processor or blender with the olive oil and vinegar, then blitz until smooth. Season to taste, and drizzle over the salads to serve.

# Brandade with griddled sourdough

Soak the salt cod for an hour or two if the fish is only lightly salted, or up to 24 hours if it is very dried out, changing the water at least twice. If in doubt check with your fishmonger or follow the instructions on the packet.

1. 150g (5oz) salt cod, soaked (see above)
2. 120ml (4fl oz) double cream
3. 2 garlic cloves, peeled
4. 1 small sourdough loaf
5. lemon wedges, to serve
&. salt and freshly ground black pepper; 120ml (4fl oz) extra-virgin olive oil, plus extra for drizzling

**serves 4–6 as a starter or for tapas**

**step one** Poach the soaked salt cod in a small pan with a little water for about 10 minutes, then drain and roughly flake the flesh, removing all the skin and bones.

**step two** Meanwhile, put the olive oil and cream in a pan and bring to the boil. Put the poached cod flesh and the garlic in a food processor and turn on. Gradually pour in the hot oil and cream mixture through the feeder tube to build up a thick emulsion.

Season to taste; you may not need any salt. Transfer to a bowl and drizzle with olive oil, then add a good grinding of pepper. Set on a large platter and set aside until needed.

**step three** Heat a griddle pan until smoking hot. Cut the sourdough into slices and cook for a minute or two on each side until lightly charred. Drizzle over a little olive oil. Arrange the sourdough around the brandade on the platter and garnish with the lemon wedges.

# Soups and salads

# Fresh tomato and smoked bacon soup

This clever soup is great in autumn when there is a glut of ripe tomatoes, but you can use canned ones. As it uses no stock it has a wonderfully intense tomato flavour with a smoky backdrop. I love to serve this soup with hunks of crusty bread, but do try it chilled on a hot summer's day.

1. 2 large onions, finely chopped
2. 350g (12oz) piece smoked bacon or pancetta, diced
3. 2 garlic cloves, peeled and finely chopped
4. 1.75kg (4lb) ripe tomatoes, roughly chopped, or 4 x 400g (14oz) cans chopped tomatoes (or use a mixture of both)
5. 2 tablespoons tomato purée
&. sea salt and freshly ground black pepper; 3 tablespoons olive oil

**serves 4–6 as a starter**

**step one** Heat 2 tablespoons of the oil in a large pan. Add the onions, bacon or pancetta and garlic and cook for about 10 minutes, stirring occasionally, or until the onions have softened and the bacon is cooked through and lightly golden.

**step two** Stir in the tomatoes and tomato purée and season to taste. Bring to a simmer and cook gently for 15–20 minutes, stirring occasionally, or until all the flavours are well combined. Blitz the soup with a hand blender or in batches in a food processor, then pass through a fine sieve.

**step three** Return the soup to a clean pan and season to taste, then reheat gently. To serve, ladle the soup into bowls and place on plates. Add a drizzle of olive oil to the top of each one with a good grinding of black pepper.

# Hint of mint garden pea soup

For a healthier option, use extra-virgin olive oil instead of the cream.

1. 2 shallots, finely chopped
2. 450g (1lb) frozen peas
3. 6 fresh mint leaves
4. 900ml (1½ pints) vegetable stock
5. 4–6 tablespoons soured cream
&. sea salt and freshly ground black pepper; 2 tablespoons olive oil

**serves 4–6 as a starter**

**step one** Heat the oil in a pan. Add the shallots and sauté for about 5 minutes, stirring occasionally, until softened but not coloured. Add the peas and mint and stir until well coated. Pour in the stock and bring to the boil. Season to taste. Simmer for 3 minutes, stirring, to allow the flavours to combine.

**step two** Blend the soup to a purée using a hand-held blender or in batches in a food processor. Return to the pan, season to taste and reheat gently.

**step three** Ladle the soup into warmed bowls. Swirl in the soured cream and add a good grinding of black pepper. Serve immediately.

# Borscht and apple soup

You can buy cooked beetroot in supermarkets, otherwise, you can cook your own (see method used for Watercress, beetroot and orange salad, page 23).

1. 2 onions, finely chopped
2. 450g (1lb) cooked beetroot, peeled and diced
3. 1 Granny Smith apple, peeled, cored and diced
4. 900ml (1½ pints) vegetable stock
5. 4–6 tablespoons crème fraîche
&. sea salt and freshly ground black pepper; 2 tablespoons olive oil

**serves 4–6 as a starter**

**step one** Heat the oil in a large pan and add the onions, stirring to combine. Cook for about 5 minutes, stirring occasionally, until softened but not coloured. Season to taste.

**step two** Add the beetroot and apple to the pan, stirring to coat, and cook for another minute or two, then pour in the stock, bring to the boil and season. Reduce the heat and simmer for 10 minutes until the beetroot and apple are completely tender.

**step three** Purée the soup with a hand blender or in batches in a food processor, then return to a clean pan and reheat gently. Season to taste, ladle the soup into bowls set on plates and swirl a spoonful of crème fraîche into each one to serve.

# Watercress, beetroot and orange salad

This salad is really lovely served with grilled sardines and crusty bread.

**1** 450g (1lb) raw beetroot, washed and dried, with the tops removed
**2** 3 large oranges
**3** 1 teaspoon white wine vinegar
**4** 100g (4oz) watercress, woody stems removed
**5** 1 small red onion, thinly sliced into rings
**&** sea salt and freshly ground black pepper; 4 tablespoons extra-virgin olive oil

*serves 4 as a starter*

**step one** Preheat the oven to 190°C/375°F/gas 5. Spread a thin layer of sea salt on a large piece of foil. Arrange the beetroot on top and seal inside the foil. Bake for 45 minutes to 1 hour until they are tender and can be pierced easily with a knife.

**step two** Meanwhile, peel two of the oranges, remove the pith and cut into segments, catching the juices in a bowl. Squeeze the juice of the third orange into a bowl. Add the white wine vinegar and oil and then whisk to combine. Season to taste.

**step three** Remove the beetroot from the oven. Unwrap the foil parcel and leave the beetroot to cool slightly. While the beetroot are still warm, peel them with a small knife, then cut into chunks or slices. Arrange the beetroot, orange segments, watercress and red onion rings on a platter or individual plates and drizzle over the dressing to serve.

# Roasted red pepper and basil salad

Cooling the peppers in a covered bowl makes them so much easier to peel.

**1** 4 large red peppers
**2** 4 large yellow peppers
**3** ½ teaspoon balsamic vinegar
**4** 1 garlic clove, peeled and crushed (optional)
**5** a handful of fresh basil leaves
**&** sea salt and freshly ground black pepper; 3 tablespoons extra-virgin olive oil

*serves 4–6 as a starter*

**step one** Preheat the grill and cook the peppers for 20–30 minutes until well charred, turning regularly. Allow to cool completely in a large bowl covered with clingfilm, then peel, catching all of the juices. Slice the flesh into strips, discarding the seeds and cores. Place in a bowl and set aside until needed.

**step two** Pour the oil into a bowl and whisk in the balsamic vinegar, reserved pepper juices and garlic, if using. Season to taste. Arrange the roasted pepper strips on a platter or individual plates and drizzle over the dressing. Roughly tear up the basil leaves and use as a garnish. Serve at room temperature.

# Eggs and cheese

# Welsh rarebit

Welsh rarebit is a great British classic, and is extremely versatile. I like to use it to cover my salmon fish pie (page 130) or simply pile on top of a dish of blanched cauliflower and bake in the oven for an interesting twist on cauliflower cheese! To make these into more of a meal, serve with salad or some wilted spinach on the side.

1 225g (8oz) vintage Cheddar cheese, grated
2 3 eggs
3 1 teaspoon prepared English mustard
4 a few drops of Worcestershire sauce
5 2 part-baked half ciabatta loaves or 4 large slices white bread
& sea salt and freshly ground black pepper

**serves 4 as a snack**

**step one** Preheat the oven to 220°C/425°F/gas 7. Put the Cheddar in a bowl. Separate the eggs and put the egg whites in a separate large bowl. Add the yolks to the Cheddar with the mustard and Worcestershire sauce. Season to taste.

**step two** Whisk the egg whites with an electric mixer until they stand in stiff peaks. Add a spoonful of the egg whites into the cheese mixture to lighten it, then gently fold in the rest of the egg whites.

**step three** If using ciabatta, cut the loaves open into two even-sized pieces or lightly toast the slices of white bread in a toaster. Arrange on a baking sheet, then share out the Welsh rarebit mixture among them. Bake for 10 minutes until risen and lightly browned. Transfer to plates, cut in half on the diagonal and serve at once.

# Filo baskets with black and blue

Black pudding and melted blue cheese is a really tasty combination. Look out for the authentic Greek filo pastry, it really is a superior product. To prevent it from drying out, cover with a damp cloth until ready to use. This recipe would also work well as bite-sized canapés, using mini muffin trays to make the baskets.

1. 50g (2oz) unsalted butter
2. 3 sheets filo pastry, thawed if frozen
3. 200g (7oz) black pudding, casing removed and cut into 8 slices
4. about 6 tablespoons onion marmalade (from a jar)
5. 100g (4oz) Cashel Blue cheese, crumbled
& 1 teaspoon sunflower oil

**serves 4 as a starter**

**step one** Preheat the oven to 180°C/350°F/gas 4. Melt the butter in a small pan or in the microwave and leave to cool.

**step two** Unfold the filo pastry and cut the sheets into quarters, then cover with a damp tea towel. Take 4 x 200ml (7fl oz) glass ramekins and turn them upside down on a non-stick baking sheet.

**step three** Take a piece of filo, brush with butter, then use to cover the top of the ramekin, buttered-side down. Add another two layers of the buttered filo pastry, placing each square at a slightly different angle. Continue until you have covered all four ramekins in this way.

**step four** Bake the filo baskets for 10–12 minutes until just cooked through and lightly golden. When cool enough to handle, carefully remove the filo baskets from the ramekins, then transfer to a wire rack and leave to cool completely.

**step five** Heat a heavy-based frying pan with the sunflower oil and sauté the black pudding for a minute or so on each side until lightly crisp.

**step six** Add a heaped tablespoon of the onion marmalade to the base of each filo basket and arrange two slices of the sliced black pudding on top. Scatter over the Cashel Blue and arrange on a baking sheet. Bake for another 5–6 minutes until the Cashel Blue is melted and bubbling. Arrange on plates and garnish each one with a teaspoon of the onion marmalade to serve.

# Caramelized onion and bacon frittata

This is one of my favourite frittatas, which originates from Sicily. The sweetness of the onions complements the smokiness of the bacon perfectly. It is as good served cold as hot or warm and makes a great light lunch or supper.

**1** 3 Spanish onions, thinly sliced
**2** 175g (6oz) piece pancetta or smoked streaky bacon, cut into small lardons
**3** 8 large eggs, beaten
**4** 50g (2oz) freshly grated Parmesan
**5** 2 tablespoons chopped fresh flat-leaf parsley
**&** salt and freshly ground black pepper; 4 tablespoons olive oil

**serves 4**

**step one** Heat half the oil in a large sauté or frying pan. Add the onions and start by cooking over a fairly high heat, stirring constantly, until they begin to soften but not brown, then reduce the heat and continue to cook over a medium heat, stirring frequently so the onions do not stick or brown. They will need about 1 hour in total to caramelize.

**step two** Stir the pancetta or bacon into the onion mixture and cook for another 3–4 minutes until it has begun to sizzle and crisp up. Tip into a large bowl and leave to cool for at least 5 minutes. Season generously.

**step three** Preheat the oven to 180°C/350°F/gas 4. Add the beaten eggs, Parmesan and parsley to the onions and stir well to combine – you should have 1.2 litres (2 pints) of mixture in total. Heat the remaining oil in an ovenproof heavy-based pan that is about 23cm (9 inches) in diameter and deep enough to take the mixture. Swirl around the oil to coat the sides of the pan evenly, then pour in the egg mixture and cook for 6–8 minutes over a low heat to set the bottom and sides.

**step four** Transfer the pan to the oven and cook, uncovered, for about 20 minutes until just set, puffed up and lightly golden. Loosen the sides with a palette knife, cut the frittata into wedges and serve warm or cold on plates. Alternatively, cut into small cubes, spear with cocktail sticks and serve as picnic food or an addition to a platter of antipasti.

# Gruyère cheese soufflé

Use a proper straight-sided soufflé dish to get the best rise. Running a knife around the edge of the mixture before it goes into the oven helps it rise more evenly. Remember when the soufflé comes out of the oven there should be a slight wobble which means it is still nice and moist in the middle. I like to serve this with a simply dressed rocket salad.

❶ 25g (1oz) butter, plus extra for greasing
❷ 2 tablespoons plain flour, plus extra for dusting
❸ 200ml (7fl oz) milk
❹ 4 large eggs
❺ 75g (3oz) Gruyère cheese, finely grated
**&** salt and freshly ground white pepper

**serves 4**

**step one** Preheat the oven to 180°C/350°F/gas 4. Grease a 1.25 litre (2 pint) soufflé dish with butter. Sprinkle the dish with flour, tilting it up the sides until the whole dish is lightly coated. Tip out any excess.

**step two** Melt the butter in a pan, then add the flour and cook for 1 minute, stirring. Remove from the heat and gradually stir in the milk until you have achieved a smooth sauce. Bring to the boil slowly and cook, stirring, until the sauce thickens. Season to taste and leave to cool slightly.

**step three** Separate the eggs and put the egg whites into a large bowl. Beat the egg yolks into the cooled sauce, one at a time. Sprinkle in the Gruyère, reserving a tablespoon for the topping. Stir the cheese into the sauce until evenly combined.

**step four** Whisk the egg whites with an electric mixer until they stand in soft peaks. Mix one large spoonful of the egg white into the sauce to lighten it. Gently pour the sauce over the remaining egg whites and, using a large metal spoon, carefully fold the ingredients together. Take care not to overmix, then gently pour into the prepared soufflé dish.

**step five** Sprinkle the reserved Gruyère over the top and quickly run a knife around the edge of the mixture. Place on a baking sheet and bake for about 30 minutes until the top is golden brown, well risen and firm to the touch. There should still be a slight wobble in the centre of the soufflé. Serve immediately, straight to the table, and allow guests to help themselves.

# Brie quesadillas

Let's do the Mexican wave as you'll be up and down getting another slice of these gorgeous treats. These quesadillas are a perfect snack anytime: me and my mates love them at half time when we're watching the footie. And you can ring the changes with all sorts of fillings. They can be prepared up to one hour in advance, covered with clingfilm and kept at room temperature. Then simply flash through the oven when you are ready to serve.

1. 8 soft flour tortillas
2. 350g (12oz) Brie, thinly sliced
3. 1 mild red chilli, seeded and finely chopped
4. 1 ripe mango, peeled, stoned and thinly sliced
5. 2 spring onions, thinly sliced
&. sea salt and freshly ground black pepper; 4 teaspoons olive oil, for brushing

**serves 4–6 as a snack**

**step one** Preheat the oven to 200°C/400°F/gas 6 and heat a ridged griddle pan over a medium heat until very hot. Brush one side of each tortilla with a little of the olive oil. Place one tortilla in the pan, oiled-side down, and cook for 1 minute until nicely marked, pressing down with a spatula. Repeat with the remaining tortillas.

**step two** Arrange half the tortillas on baking sheets, marked-side down. Place a layer of Brie on top and then scatter over the chilli, mango and spring onions. Season to taste.

Cover with the remaining tortillas, marked-side up, and bake for about 5 minutes or until heated through and the Brie has melted. Allow the quesadillas to cool slightly for ease of handling, then cut each one into eight wedges with a serrated knife, pizza cutter or kitchen scissors. Arrange on warmed plates or one large platter to serve.

# Pasta, pulses and grains

These are the basis of so many good meals and just need a few choice ingredients to bring them to life. We all stick to our favourites, but some of the less familiar ones will really inspire you.

# Pasta shapes

# Strozzapreti with creamy pesto chicken

Pasta is a great standby for those evenings when you have absolutely no time to cook. It's important to remember to stir it once to separate the pasta and to cook at a rolling boil to prevent it from sticking. Strozzapreti is a hand-rolled elongated pasta from Emilia-Romagna, Tuscany and Umbria, and it's available in single and tri-coloured versions. If you cannot find any, you can substitute another pasta shape.

1. 350g (12oz) strozzapreti tris (tri-coloured) pasta
2. 225g (8oz) mini chicken fillets, cut into bite-sized pieces
3. 300ml (½ pint) double cream
4. 4 tablespoons ready-made pesto (good quality)
5. 6 tablespoons freshly grated Parmesan
& salt and freshly ground black pepper; 1 tablespoon olive oil

**serves 4**

**step one** Bring a large pan of water to a rolling boil and add a good pinch of salt. Add the strozzapreti, stir once, and cook for 15 minutes, or according to the packet instructions, until the pasta is al dente.

**step two** Meanwhile, heat the olive oil in a heavy-based frying pan. Add the chicken pieces, season generously and sauté for 2–3 minutes until well sealed and lightly golden on all sides. Stir in the cream and allow to bubble down, then lower the heat and simmer until reduced by one-third. Stir in the pesto and season to taste. The chicken should now be cooked through and tender.

**step three** Drain the pasta in a colander and return to the pan. Tip in the chicken and pesto cream, stirring to combine, then fold in two-thirds of the Parmesan. Share among warmed pasta bowls and scatter the remaining Parmesan on top with a grind or two of pepper to serve.

# Penne with chargrilled artichokes, roasted red peppers and spinach

This recipe is really stunning and a great vegetarian option. Use the best chargrilled artichokes you can find; look for the Italian wood-fired ones, which have a wonderful smoky flavour, and the oil is so good it seems a shame not to use it!

1. 2 red peppers
2. 350g (12oz) penne pasta
3. 1 x 175g (6oz) jar chargrilled artichoke hearts preserved in olive oil
4. 1 red onion, thinly sliced
5. 100g (4oz) tender young spinach leaves
&. salt and freshly ground black pepper

**serves 4**

**step one** Preheat the grill. Halve the peppers and place them, cut-side down, on the rack of the grill pan. Grill for 10–15 minutes until the skin is blackened and charred. Place in a large bowl, cover with clingfilm and leave to cool. Once they are cool enough to handle, remove the skin, cores and seeds, then cut the flesh into slices. Set aside.

**step two** Bring a large pan of water to a rolling boil and add a good pinch of salt. Add the penne, stir once, and cook for 10–12 minutes, or according to the packet instructions, until the pasta is al dente.

**step three** Meanwhile, drain the olive oil from the artichokes into a large frying pan over a medium heat. Add the onion and sauté for 3–4 minutes until softened but not coloured. Cut the artichoke hearts into quarters and add to the pan with the red pepper strips, tossing to combine.

**step four** Tip the spinach into the frying pan and allow to just wilt down, then remove the pan from the heat. Season to taste.

**step five** Drain the pasta and add the vegetable and oil mixture, stirring well to combine. Share among warmed pasta bowls and serve at once.

# Pumpkin pancetta penne

Look out for small organic pumpkins, which are normally a vibrant orange, as their size is perfect for this recipe. Once the pumpkin is peeled and seeded you should end up with just over 450g (1lb) of the flesh.

**1** 500g (1lb 2oz) penne or rigatoni pasta
**2** 175g (6oz) pancetta, cubed, or smoked streaky bacon lardons
**3** 800g (1lb 12oz) small pumpkin, peeled, seeded and finely diced
**4** 4 tablespoons finely shredded fresh sage leaves
**5** 50g (2oz) freshly grated Parmesan, plus extra to garnish
**&** sea salt and freshly ground black pepper; 4 tablespoons olive oil

**serves 6**

**step one** Bring a large pan of water to a rolling boil and add a good pinch of salt. Add the penne or rigatoni, stir once, and cook for 10–12 minutes or according to the packet instructions, until the pasta is al dente.

**step two** Heat the olive oil in a heavy-based pan then add the pancetta or smoked streaky bacon lardons. Cook for 2–3 minutes, stirring occasionally, until the pancetta begins to go crispy.

**step three** Add the pumpkin to the pan with the sage and mix well to combine. Season to taste and cook for 4–5 minutes, stirring occasionally, until the pumpkin is cooked through but still holding its shape.

**step four** Drain the pasta and add to the pumpkin with the crispy pancetta. Stir in the Parmesan and then season to taste. To serve, share among warmed pasta bowls and top each one with a sprinkling of Parmesan and a good grinding of pepper.

# Orecchiette with ham and petits pois

This is a great pasta dish for when I've got some leftover ham – or even rare roast beef – in the fridge. It really takes no time to prepare and is very satisfying to eat on a cold winter's night. Orecchiette is a type of pasta from Apulia in southern Italy, which is about 2cm (¾ inch) across, and with its small white dome and a centre thinner than its edge, roughly resembles a small ear. However, small pasta shells make a good alternative.

**❶** 350g (12oz) orecchiette pasta
**❷** 175g (6oz) frozen petits pois
**❸** 175g (6oz) piece of cooked ham, diced
**❹** 2 tablespoons creamed horseradish
**❺** 4 tablespoons roughly chopped fresh flat-leaf parsley
**&** salt and freshly ground black pepper; 3 tablespoons extra-virgin olive oil

**serves 4**

**step one** Bring a large pan of water to a rolling boil and add a good pinch of salt. Add the orecchiette, stir once, and cook for 15 minutes, or according to the packet instructions, until the pasta is al dente.

**step two** Meanwhile, cook the petits pois in a separate pan of boiling salted water for 2–3 minutes until tender.

**step three** Drain the pasta into a colander and return to the pan. Drain the peas and add to the pasta with the ham, horseradish, parsley and olive oil. Stir and toss well to combine and season to taste. Cook over a gentle heat until just warmed through, then share among warmed pasta bowls to serve.

# Smoked salmon tagliatelle with Parmesan cream

It's amazing how such a simple dish can turn out so stylishly! For convenience use ready-sliced smoked salmon. There is a general rule that you should never add Parmesan to a fish-based pasta dish, but this recipe is an exception.

1. 350g (12oz) egg tagliatelle (good quality)
2. 200g (7oz) sliced smoked salmon
3. 4 tablespoons torn or finely sliced fresh basil, plus extra to garnish
4. 300ml (½ pint) double cream
5. 6 tablespoons freshly grated Parmesan, plus extra to garnish
& sea salt and freshly ground black pepper

**serves 4**

**step one** Bring a large pan of water to a rolling boil and add a good pinch of salt. Add the tagliatelle and cook for 10–12 minutes (give it a stir after 3–5 minutes) or according to the packet instructions, until the pasta is al dente.

**step two** Meanwhile, cut the smoked salmon into long strips and mix with the basil. Pour the cream into a pan and bring to the boil, then boil for 2–3 minutes, stirring occasionally, until thickened. Remove from the heat and stir in the Parmesan, then season with pepper. The heat of the cream should melt the cheese perfectly.

**step three** Drain the pasta and toss with the Parmesan cream, fork in the smoked salmon and basil mixture until well combined. Share among warmed pasta bowls and garnish with the remaining Parmesan and basil to serve.

# Spaghetti

# Spaghetti with fiery broccoli and anchovies

There are now three different types of broccoli: calabrese with a single, compact, dense head similar to a cauliflower; purple sprouting broccoli with lots of small florets, commonly known in Italy as broccoletti; and the long- stemmed variety with small bright green leaves along the stems. All would work perfectly well in this spaghetti dish.

**1** 400g (14oz) purple sprouting broccoli, trimmed and cut into small florets
**2** 350g (12oz) spaghetti
**3** 1 x 50g (2oz) can anchovy fillets, drained
**4** 2 garlic cloves, peeled and thinly sliced
**5** 2 long red chillies, seeded and thinly sliced
**&** salt and freshly ground black pepper; 6 tablespoons olive oil

**serves 4**

**step one** Bring two large pans of water to a rolling boil and add a good pinch of salt. Drop the broccoli into one pan and cook for 2–3 minutes, or until just tender, then drain and quickly refresh under cold running water to prevent it from cooking any further. Swirl the spaghetti into the other pan, stir once, and cook for 10–12 minutes or according to the packet instructions until the pasta is al dente.

**step two** Meanwhile place the anchovies in a large frying pan with the oil. Cook over a low heat, mashing with a wooden spoon until they have almost completely disintegrated. Add the garlic and chilli and cook for another minute, stirring. Add the broccoli to the pan and increase the heat. Cook for 1–2 minutes or until just heated through, tossing occasionally.

**step three** Drain the pasta, then return to the pan and add the broccoli mixture, tossing well to combine. Share between warmed pasta bowls and top with a good grinding of black pepper before serving.

# Spaghetti with walnut and pecorino pesto

This pesto makes a nice change from your average basil version but is only as good as the walnuts you use so do make sure they are really fresh. It is also delicious swirled into tomato soup or try stuffing some underneath the skin of a chicken breast before roasting. I also like to use it as a dressing for salads or spread onto crostini and topped with bubbling goats' cheese.

1 50g (2oz) shelled walnuts
2 25g (1oz) fresh flat-leaf parsley leaves
3 2 garlic cloves, peeled and roughly chopped
4 50g (2oz) freshly grated pecorino cheese, plus extra to garnish
5 350g (12oz) spaghetti
& sea salt and freshly ground black pepper; 120ml (4fl oz) extra-virgin olive oil

**serves 4**

**step one** Preheat the oven to 180°C/350°F/gas 4. Spread the walnuts out on a baking sheet and roast for 8–10 minutes until lightly toasted. Remove from the oven and leave to cool completely.

**step two** Put the parsley in a food processor with 1 teaspoon of the salt and the garlic, then blend until finely minced. Add the cooled walnuts and the pecorino cheese and blitz again briefly, then, with the machine running, pour in the olive oil through the feeder tube until the pesto is thickened and emulsified. Season to taste.

**step three** Bring a large pan of water to a rolling boil and add a good pinch of salt. Swirl in the spaghetti, stir once, and cook for 10–12 minutes or according to the packet instructions until the pasta is al dente. Drain, then tip back into the pan and pour in the pesto. Stir until all the spaghetti is well coated in the sauce, then divide among warmed pasta bowls. Sprinkle over some pecorino and serve at once.

# Spaghetti with spicy tomato sauce and crispy chorizo

If you buy a good-quality chorizo you really don't need much to flavour this tomato-based pasta sauce. Look out for Iberian chorizo made from the highest quality acorn-fed Iberian pigs, reared outdoors in the Dehesa area of western Spain.

1. 350g (12oz) spaghetti
2. 75g (3oz) thinly sliced cooked chorizo, cut into strips
3. 2 garlic cloves, peeled and finely chopped
4. ½ teaspoon dried chilli flakes
5. 400ml (14fl oz) passata (Italian sieved tomatoes)
& salt and freshly ground black pepper; 2 tablespoons olive oil

**serves 4**

**step one** Bring a large pan of water to a rolling boil and add a good pinch of salt. Swirl in the spaghetti, stir once, and cook for 10–12 minutes or according to the packet instructions until the pasta is al dente.

**step two** Meanwhile, heat the olive oil in a sauté pan and fry the chorizo for a couple of minutes until it has begun to release its oil and become crispy. Remove with a slotted spoon, leaving as much of the red chorizo oil in the pan as possible, then set aside on a plate until needed.

**step three** Add the garlic to the pan with the chilli flakes and cook for about 20 seconds, stirring. Pour in the passata and cook for 3–4 minutes until slightly reduced and thickened. Season to taste.

**step four** When the pasta is cooked, drain and return to the pan. Pour in the tomato mixture and add most of the crispy chorizo, reserving some to garnish. Then fold everything together until well combined. Share among warmed pasta bowls and garnish with the reserved crispy chorizo to serve.

# Spaghetti with smoked chicken, rocket and cherry tomatoes

So simple a dish yet deliciously satisfying.

❶ 350g (12oz) spaghetti
❷ 2 large garlic cloves, peeled and finely chopped
❸ 275g (10oz) cherry tomatoes, halved
❹ 175g (6oz) cooked smoked chicken breast, skinned and cut into strips
❺ 75g (3oz) wild rocket
& salt and freshly ground black pepper; 4 tablespoons extra-virgin olive oil

serves 4

**step one** Bring a large pan of water to a rolling boil, and add a good pinch of salt. Swirl in the spaghetti, stir once, and cook for 10–12 minutes or according to the packet instructions until the pasta is al dente.

**step two** Heat half the olive oil in a large frying pan and quickly sauté the garlic for 20–30 seconds until sizzling but not coloured. Tip in the cherry tomatoes, then season generously and continue to sauté for 2–3 minutes until slightly charred but just holding their shape.

**step three** Drain the spaghetti and return to the pan, then fold in the cherry tomato mixture with the smoked chicken and rocket until just heated through. Share among warmed pasta bowls and top with a good grinding of black pepper before serving.

# Spaghetti alle vongole in bianco

This recipe originates from Naples where it is still traditionally eaten on Christmas Eve – a day of fasting in the Italian calendar. Look out for amande, palourde or telline clams for the best flavour and make sure that they're spanking fresh before buying them.

❶ 350g (12oz) spaghetti
❷ 1.75kg (4lb) small clams
❸ 2 garlic cloves, peeled and finely chopped
❹ a good pinch of dried chilli flakes
❺ 1 tablespoon chopped fresh flat-leaf parsley
& salt; 150ml (¼ pint) extra-virgin olive oil

**serves 4**

**step one** Bring a large pan of water to a rolling boil and add a good pinch of salt. Swirl in the spaghetti, stir once, and cook for 10–12 minutes or according to the packet instructions until the pasta is al dente.

**step two** Wash the clams thoroughly in a bowl under cold running water to get rid of all of the sand in the shells. Discard any that do not close when sharply tapped.

**step three** Heat the olive oil in a large sauté pan with a lid and sauté the garlic for 10–20 seconds until sizzling but not coloured. Add the clams, give the pan a good shake and cover with a lid. Cook for a couple of minutes until the shells open and then immediately remove from the heat.

**step four** Remove the clams from the pan with a slotted spoon, discarding any that have not opened. Reserve about half of the clams in their shells and take the remainder out of their shells. Return all of the clams to the cooking liquid in the sauté pan and add the chilli flakes and parsley.

**step five** Drain the spaghetti and then tip into the clam mixture. Stir over a gentle heat for a minute or two so that the pasta absorbs the broth and flavour of the clams. Season to taste and share among warmed pasta bowls and serve at once.

# Pulses
# and grains

# Roasted red and yellow pepper couscous

Try not to crowd the veg in the roasting tin as they'll stew rather than roast.

**1** 2 red peppers, halved, seeded and cut into 2.5cm (1 inch) squares
**2** 2 yellow peppers, halved, seeded and cut into 2.5cm (1 inch) squares
**3** 1 large red onion, cut into 2.5cm (1 inch) pieces
**4** a handful of fresh basil leaves, chopped
**5** 225g (8oz) couscous
**&** sea salt and freshly ground black pepper; 6 tablespoons extra-virgin olive oil

**serves 4**

**step one** Preheat the oven to 220°C/425°F/gas 7 and heat a large roasting tin. Coat the peppers and onion with 2 tablespoons of oil. Tip into the heated roasting tin, season generously and roast for 30–40 minutes until completely tender and lightly caramelized, tossing occasionally. Five minutes before they are ready, combine the chopped basil with the vegetables and return to the oven.

**step two** Place the couscous in a large bowl. Drizzle over the remaining oil, stirring gently to combine. Pour over 225ml (8fl oz) boiling water, stir well, cover and leave to stand for 5 minutes before separating the grains with a fork. Season to taste and reheat gently in a pan, stirring continuously with a fork. Fold in the roasted red and yellow pepper mixture, then share out on warmed plates to serve.

# Puy lentil salad with sun-dried tomatoes and goats' cheese

This is one of my favourite salads and will keep well in the fridge.

**1** 225g (8oz) Puy lentils, rinsed in cold water
**2** 2 shallots, finely sliced
**3** 50g (2oz) sun-dried tomatoes preserved in olive oil, drained
**4** 175g (6oz) goats' cheese log, cut into small cubes
**5** 25g (1oz) roughly chopped fresh flat-leaf parsley
**&** sea salt and freshly ground black pepper; 4 tablespoons extra-virgin olive oil

**serves 4**

**step one** Place the lentils in a pan with 600ml (1 pint) of salted water. Bring to the boil, then lower the heat and simmer for 15–20 minutes or until just tender. Drain well.

**step two** Meanwhile, heat 1 tablespoon of the olive oil in a frying pan and sauté the shallots for 4–5 minutes until softened but not coloured. Tip into a salad bowl and stir in the cooked lentils with the rest of the olive oil and the sun-dried tomatoes and leave to cool.

**step three** When the lentils have cooled to room temperature, gently fold in the goats' cheese and parsley, then season to taste and serve at once.

# Sausage, tomato and butter bean bake

Butter beans originate from Greece and are simply delicious served with good-quality sausages. There is now a fantastic selection available and you can choose from fresh chorizo, venison or a more traditional pork and leek. Haricot or borlotti beans would also work well for this dish, as would a little chilli and garlic in the tomato sauce.

**1** 6–8 large butcher-style pork sausages
**2** 1 large onion, finely chopped
**3** 1 tablespoon chopped fresh sage
**4** 1 x 400g (14oz) can chopped tomatoes
**5** 2 x 400g (14oz) cans butter beans, drained and rinsed
**&** salt and freshly ground black pepper; 4 tablespoons extra-virgin olive oil

**serves 3 or 4**

**step one** Preheat the oven to 180°C/350°F/ gas 4. Heat 1 tablespoon of the oil in a large, heavy-based frying pan. Add the sausages and cook gently for 1–2 minutes or until just sealed and lightly browned on both sides. Transfer to a plate and set aside.

**step two** Wipe out the frying pan and then add the remaining olive oil. Tip in the onion and sage and sauté very gently for about 10 minutes until the onion is completely softened but not coloured. Add the tomatoes, bring to a simmer, then cook for about 5 minutes, stirring occasionally until the sauce is slightly reduced and thickened. Then season to taste.

**step three** Transfer the tomato mixture to an oven dish and stir in the butter beans, then arrange the sausages on top, burying them into the mixture. Roast for 15–20 minutes until the butter beans are bubbling and the sausages are cooked through and tender. Serve straight to the table and allow everyone to tuck in.

# Roasted haddock on chickpea and chorizo sauté

The chickpea and chorizo sauté will keep well in the fridge for up to two days.

1. 4 x 150g (5oz) skinless haddock fillets, pin bones removed
2. 1 large red onion, finely chopped
3. 2 raw chorizo sausages, skinned and finely diced (about 100g (4oz) in total)
4. 2 x 400g (14oz) cans chickpeas, drained and rinsed
5. 15g (½oz) roughly chopped fresh coriander leaves
& salt and freshly ground black pepper; 4 tablespoons extra-virgin olive oil

**serves 4**

**step one** Preheat the oven to 200°C/400°F/gas 6. Place the haddock fillets on a non-stick baking sheet, season, then drizzle over 1 tablespoon of oil. Roast for 10–12 minutes or until just tender but moist in the middle.

**step two** Heat 1 tablespoon of the oil in a large sauté pan. Add the onion and sauté for 3–4 minutes until softened but not coloured. Tip in the chorizo and cook for another few minutes until the colour has started to bleed into the onion. Add the chickpeas to the pan and sauté for another few minutes until the chickpeas are completely heated through. Stir in the coriander with the remaining oil and season to taste. Share among warmed bowls with roasted haddock on top of each one to serve.

# Tabbouleh salad

This gorgeous, colourful Middle Eastern salad is great with barbecued food.

1. 100g (4oz) bulgur wheat
2. juice of 1 lemon
3. 4 ripe vine tomatoes, halved, seeded and diced
4. 25g (1oz) roughly chopped fresh flat-leaf parsley
5. 1 bunch spring onions, trimmed and finely chopped
& sea salt and freshly ground black pepper; 6 tablespoons extra-virgin olive oil

**serves 4**

**step one** Cover the bulgur wheat with cold water. Set aside for 45 minutes, or according to the packet instructions, until just tender. Rinse well, drain and tip into a salad bowl.

**step two** Meanwhile, season the lemon juice to taste and mix until the salt has dissolved. Combine with the olive oil.

**step three** Add the tomatoes, parsley and spring onions to the drained bulgur wheat. Season to taste and set aside at room temperature to allow the flavours to develop.

**step four** Just before serving, pour over the dressing and give the salad a quick mix.

# Vegetarian dishes

You don't need to pile up the ingredients to create tasty vegetarian meals. Get to know the flavour combinations that work for you and you'll soon be cooking delicious dishes that pack a veggie punch. Don't forget to look in the two previous chapters for more veggie ideas.

# Vegetarian

# Hash browns with soft poached eggs and roasted cherry tomatoes

Hash browns are an irresistible addition to any cooked breakfast but I also like them as a light supper. If you're not vegetarian, try adding 75g (3oz) of finely chopped pancetta that has been sautéed first to the potato mixture.

1. 900g (2lb) potatoes (e.g. Maris Piper or King Edwards), scrubbed (even-sized)
2. 4 cherry tomato vines, each with 5–7 tomatoes
3. 25g (1oz) butter
4. 1 tablespoon white wine vinegar
5. 4 large eggs
&. salt and freshly ground black pepper; 1 tablespoon olive oil

serves 4

**step one** Preheat the oven to 180°C/350°F/gas 4. Cook the potatoes in a pan of salted water for approximately 15 minutes until almost tender. Drain and leave until cool enough to handle, then peel. Coarsely grate the potatoes and season generously.

**step two** Place the tomato vines in a small roasting tin and drizzle with half the olive oil. Roast for 18–20 minutes until the tomatoes are tender and the skins have split.

**step three** Heat the rest of the oil and the butter in a large, heavy-based frying pan. Shape the potato mixture into four patties and add to the pan. Turn down the heat and cook for 10 minutes until lightly golden, then turn over and cook for another 10 minutes until crisp and golden brown.

**step four** Meanwhile, heat 4cm (1½ inches) of water in a separate, large, deep frying pan until little bubbles begin to appear on the surface. Add the white wine vinegar and ½ teaspoon salt. Break an egg into a teacup and then slide it gently into the water. Repeat with the other three eggs. Simmer gently for 3½ minutes until lightly poached.

**step five** Place the cooked hash browns on warmed plates. Lift the poached eggs out of the water with a slotted spoon and drain briefly on kitchen paper, then put one on each hash brown. Arrange a roasted cherry tomato vine to the side of each plate to serve.

# Paprika halloumi with roasted lemon peppers and pitta

Halloumi is a semi-hard cheese that originated in Cyprus but is now widely available. I like it pan-fried or grilled as it always retains its shape and has a lovely, soft, springy texture. It can also be brushed with olive oil and cooked on the barbie as a good veggie option. To enjoy halloumi at its best eat quickly after cooking.

**1** 4 large red peppers (or a jar of roasted peppers in olive oil)
**2** 1 lemon, halved and pips removed
**3** 250g (9oz) halloumi cheese
**4** 1 teaspoon sweet or smoked paprika
**5** 4 white pitta breads
**&** salt and freshly ground black pepper; 3 tablespoons extra-virgin olive oil

**serves 4 as a starter**

**step one** If using fresh peppers, preheat the oven to 220°C/425°F/gas 7. Arrange the red peppers in a roasting tin and cook for 20–30 minutes until well charred and blistered. Transfer to a large bowl and cover with clingfilm. Leave the peppers to cool completely, then peel, using a bowl underneath to catch all of the juices.

**step two** Slice the peppers into thick strips, discarding the seeds and cores. Place in the bowl with the pepper juices and add 2 tablespoons of olive oil or the oil from the jar of roasted peppers if using, and a squeeze of lemon juice. Season to taste and stir until well combined. Set aside until needed.

**step three** When ready to cook the halloumi, heat a griddle pan or a frying pan until very hot. Cut the halloumi cheese into four thick slices, then dust all over with the paprika.

Add the remaining oil to the hot pan and cook the halloumi for 3–4 minutes, turning once, until golden. Remove from the heat and squeeze over the remaining lemon juice.

**step four** Immediately arrange the pitta bread on the heated pan and cook for 1 minute, turning once or until puffed up and lightly charred. Cut into slices on the diagonal. Spoon the roasted pepper salad into the centre of plates and arrange a piece of the grilled halloumi on top, spooning over the lemon-flavoured pan juices. Arrange the griddled pitta slices on the side to serve.

# Baked, buttered basmati and farmhouse vegetable pilaf

I love rice cooked in this way, as it is so tasty and needs little attention. Obviously I'm limited here to the amount of ingredients I can use but you could add a couple of pinches of saffron if you've got some in the house. The frozen vegetables really don't need much cooking at all and happily steam through in just 5 minutes with the heat from the rice.

**1** 50g (2oz) butter
**2** 1 onion, finely chopped
**3** 225g (8oz) basmati rice, rinsed
**4** 600ml (1 pint) hot vegetable stock
**5** 450g (1lb) packet frozen mixed farmhouse vegetables
**&** salt and freshly ground black pepper

serves 4

**step one** Preheat the oven to 180°C/350°F/gas 4. Heat the butter in a casserole dish with a lid. Add the onion and cook for 4–5 minutes until softened but not coloured.

**step two** Tip the rice into the dish and stir well to coat it in the butter, and then pour in the stock and season to taste. Stir well, then cover with the lid and place in the oven to cook for 20 minutes until the rice is almost tender and most of the stock has been absorbed, stirring occasionally.

**step three** Remove the casserole from the oven, take off the lid and tip in the frozen vegetables. Cover again and return to the oven for 5 minutes so that the vegetables steam through and the rice is completely tender. Remove the lid and gently fold the vegetables into the rice. Pile onto warmed plates to serve.

# Creamed corn and parmesan risotto

This risotto is surprisingly rich and creamy and full of flavour yet deceptively simple. It is a favourite in our house, especially with the children. I have been known to throw in 3 or 4 handfuls of frozen peas to extend it when one or two of their hungry mates suddenly appear at teatime. If you're not able to get creamed corn, just blitz down a drained can of sweetcorn niblets with a tablespoon of cream in a food processor.

1. 1 onion, finely chopped
2. 350g (12oz) risotto rice (Carnaroli or Arborio)
3. 1.2 litres (2 pints) vegetable stock
4. 1 x 400g (14oz) can creamed sweetcorn
5. 6 tablespoons freshly grated Parmesan, plus extra to garnish
& salt and freshly ground black pepper; 2 tablespoons olive oil

**serves 4–6**

**step one** Heat the oil in a large, shallow pan. Add the onion and cook gently for about 4–5 minutes, stirring occasionally, until softened but not coloured. Increase the heat, stir in the rice and cook gently for 1 minute, stirring, until the rice is opaque.

**step two** Meanwhile, pour the stock into a separate pan and bring to a gentle simmer.

**step three** Add a ladleful of the simmering stock to the pan, stirring continuously until all the liquid has been absorbed. Continue adding ladlefuls of the stock, stirring all the time and making sure that the previous addition has been almost absorbed before adding the next.

**step four** After about 15–20 minutes, by which time the rice will be nearly cooked, tip the creamed sweetcorn into the remaining stock and simmer for 2 minutes before adding to the risotto. When the risotto is ready it should be just tender but still al dente. Season to taste, then stir in the Parmesan until combined. Ladle into warmed wide-rimmed bowls and grate over some more Parmesan to serve.

# Red pepper risotto with bubbling Camembert

The trick of a good risotto is to add the stock little by little, allowing the liquid to be almost completely absorbed before adding the next ladleful. This risotto has an amazing colour and with the bubbling cheese served on top it would be a fantastic dinner party dish. You could easily use a jar of chargrilled peppers to really speed things up.

1. 3 red peppers
2. 1 litre (1¾ pints) vegetable stock
3. 1 onion, finely chopped
4. 350g (12oz) risotto rice (Carnaroli or Arborio)
5. 2 x 150g (5oz) petit Camembert or individual goats' cheese (rind on)
&. salt and freshly ground black pepper; 5 tablespoons olive oil, plus extra for drizzling

**serves 4–6**

**step one** Preheat the grill. Cut the peppers in half and remove the seeds, stalk and inner membrane. Sprinkle a roasting tin with salt and a drizzle of the olive oil. Place the peppers, cut-side down, in the tin and drizzle over a little more oil on top. Cook under the grill for about 10 minutes or until the skins are blackened and blistered.

**step two** Transfer the pepper halves to a bowl with tongs and cover with clingfilm – this will help the skins to steam off. Leave to cool completely, then peel away the skins and discard.

**step three** Roughly chop the pepper flesh and place in a food processor. Blend while pouring 3 tablespoons of the olive oil in through the feeder tube to make a smooth purée. Transfer to a jug and cover with clingfilm. Set aside until needed.

**step four** Heat the stock in a pan and bring to a gentle simmer. Heat a heavy-based pan. Add 2 tablespoons of the oil, then add the onion and cook for 2–3 minutes, stirring, until softened but not coloured. Stir in the rice and cook for 30 seconds to 1 minute, until the oil has been absorbed and the rice grains are translucent.

**step five** Add a ladleful of the simmering stock to the pan, stirring continuously until all the liquid has been absorbed. Continue adding ladlefuls of the stock, stirring all the time, and making sure that the previous addition has been almost absorbed before adding the next. After about 18 minutes, when the rice is nearly cooked, stir in the red pepper purée and cook for a few more minutes, still stirring.

**step six** Meanwhile, cut each Camembert or goats' cheese in half and drizzle over a little olive oil with a good grinding of black pepper. Place under the grill for 2–3 minutes until bubbling. Taste the rice, it should be just cooked (al dente), and then season to taste. Ladle into warmed, wide-rimmed bowls and sit a piece of the bubbling cheese on top of each one to serve.

# Mushrooms

# Baked field mushrooms going nuts with Cashel Blue

Obviously these are fantastic served with some crusty bread to mop up all of the delicious juices but you could also serve them on a bed of mashed potato with roasted garlic for a more substantial vegetarian main course.

1. 4 large flat field or Portobello mushrooms, stalks removed
2. ½ teaspoon chopped fresh thyme
3. 2 garlic cloves, peeled and finely chopped
4. 2 tablespoons pine nuts
5. 100g (4oz) Cashel Blue, crumbled
&. sea salt and freshly ground black pepper; 2 tablespoons olive oil, plus extra for greasing

**serves 4 as a starter**

**step one** Preheat the oven to 200°C/400°F/gas 6. Arrange the mushrooms, gill-side up, in a small, lightly oiled roasting tin. Scatter over the thyme, garlic and pine nuts. Season to taste and dot over the Cashel Blue cheese, then drizzle over the olive oil.

**step two** Cover the mushrooms loosely with tin foil and roast for 15 minutes, then remove the foil and roast for 2–3 minutes until the mushrooms are completely tender and the cheese is bubbling. Transfer each mushroom to a warmed plate and spoon over the pan juices to serve.

# Garlic mushroom parcels

Use any variety of mushrooms you fancy for this recipe. There is no need to wash commercially produced ones as they are grown on sterile material. Just a quick wipe with a damp cloth will do if needed. For a lovely golden finish, brush the pastry with a little beaten egg before the parcels go into the oven.

❶ 1 x 500g (1lb 2oz) pack all-butter puff pastry, thawed if frozen
❷ plain flour, for dusting
❸ 4 teaspoons wholegrain mustard
❹ 4 garlic cloves, peeled and finely chopped
❺ 900g (2lb) chestnut mushrooms, trimmed and sliced
❽ sea salt and freshly ground black pepper; 2 tablespoons olive oil

**serves 4**

**step one** Preheat the oven to 220°C/425°F/gas 7. Cut the pastry into two and roll each piece out on a lightly floured board to a 27.5cm (11 inch) square. Cut in half and then in half again so that you end up with 4 x 13.75cm (5½ inch) squares. Transfer to two non stick baking sheets and then brush 1 teaspoon of the mustard over each one, leaving a 1cm (½ inch) border around the edges. Place in the fridge to rest for 20 minutes.

**step two** Heat the olive oil in a large frying pan. Add the garlic and mushrooms and season to taste, then sauté for 5–6 minutes until the mushrooms are completely tender and all the excess liquid has evaporated. Remove from the heat and leave to cool.

**step three** Pile the garlic mushrooms on one side of each pastry square and lightly brush around the edges with water, then fold over the pastry to enclose the filling. Press the edges firmly to seal, then flute with the back of a knife or fork. Prick the tops with a fork and transfer the baking sheets to the oven. Bake for 20–25 minutes or until puffed up and golden brown. Transfer the parcels to warmed plates to serve.

# Wild mushrooms on my croûtes

Use any selection of wild mushrooms available in the supermarket. There are now some great variety packs to look out for. Of course, many of the mushrooms are not wild in the strictest sense of the word but cultivated to make them more readily available. These are great as a starter but how about making them for brunch with a Bloody Mary?

**1** 1 French baguette
**2** 50g (2oz) butter
**3** 450g (1lb) mixed wild mushrooms, trimmed and sliced (e.g. chanterelle, cep, shiitake, oyster or morel)
**4** ½ lemon, pips removed
**5** 2 tablespoons chopped fresh flat-leaf parsley
**&** sea salt and freshly ground black pepper; 1 teaspoon sunflower oil

**serves 4 as a starter**

**step one** Preheat the oven to 200°C/400°F/gas 6. Thickly slice the baguette on the diagonal and arrange on a baking sheet. Spread each slice with some of the butter and place in the oven for 6–8 minutes until crisp and lightly golden.

**step two** Heat the oil with a knob of the butter in a frying pan. Tip in the mushrooms and sauté for 2–3 minutes over a moderate heat. Season lightly, add the remaining butter and continue to sauté for another 1–2 minutes until the mushrooms are just cooked through and tender.

**step three** Add a good squeeze of lemon juice, tip in the parsley and toss until evenly coated. Remove the croûtes from the oven and arrange on a platter or individual plates. Spoon over the wild mushrooms and serve at once.

# Chargrilled mushroom and goats' cheese burgers on sourdough bruschetta

A delicious combination of mushrooms stuffed with creamy goats' cheese, this makes a meat-free meal full of interesting flavours and textures. It is also perfect for cooking on the barbecue. If you prefer, you can substitute any soft cream cheese for the goats' cheese.

1. 8 flat field or Portobello mushrooms (select even-sized ones, about 10cm (4 inches) in diameter), stalks removed
2. 2 garlic cloves
3. 225g (8oz) soft goats' cheese
4. 1 teaspoon chopped fresh thyme
5. 4 thick slices sourdough bread (preferably a day old)
& sea salt and freshly ground black pepper; about 4 tablespoons olive oil

**serves 4**

**step one** Heat a ridged griddle pan until smoking hot. Brush with some olive oil and place the mushrooms, gill-side down, in the pan. Cook for 5 minutes or until the gills are tender, but do not turn them.

**step two** Peel and crush one of the garlic cloves and mix in a bowl with the goats' cheese and thyme, then season generously. Remove the mushrooms from the heat and brush all over with olive oil. Fill four of them with the goats' cheese mixture, and then place the remaining mushrooms on top to form sandwiches.

**step three** Give the griddle pan a quick wipe and then add the sourdough slices. Cook for 1–2 minutes on each side, until nicely marked. Cut the remaining garlic clove in half and rub all over the bread, then drizzle lightly with olive oil. Arrange on warmed plates.

**step four** Brush the mushroom burgers lightly with olive oil and put back on the griddle pan. Cook for another 3–4 minutes, turning occasionally, or until the mushrooms are cooked through and the goats' cheese starts to melt out through the sides. Place one on top of each piece of bruschetta to serve.

# Mushroom and spinach pizza

Irish soda farls make surprisingly good pizza bases as they are soft and doughy. These are fabulous made for a late-night snack or a quick wicked brunch. The sun-dried tomato paste has a lovely intense flavour, but you could use ordinary tomato purée.

① 225g (8oz) chestnut mushrooms, trimmed and sliced
② 100g (4oz) tender young spinach leaves
③ 4 soda farls
④ 4 tablespoons sun-dried tomato paste
⑤ 2 x 100g (4oz) balls buffalo mozzarella, cut into cubes or torn into pieces
& sea salt and freshly ground black pepper; 6 tablespoons olive oil

**serves 4 as a snack**

**step one** Preheat the oven to 180°C/350°F/gas 4. Heat a frying pan and then add 2 tablespoons of the olive oil. Tip in the mushrooms, season to taste and sauté for a few minutes until just tender, then add the spinach and allow it to just wilt down; this should only take a minute or so.

**step two** Meanwhile, split the soda farls in half and place on a baking sheet. Place the sun-dried tomato paste in a bowl and stir in the remaining olive oil. Spread over the cut side of the soda farls, then sprinkle with the mushroom and spinach mixture.

**step three** Scatter the mozzarella pieces over the top and bake in the oven for 8–10 minutes until the soda farls are heated through and the mozzarella is melted. Cut each pizza in half and arrange on warmed plates to serve.

# Meat and poultry

Simplicity is often the key for meat and poultry, especially if you begin with good-quality produce. There are two chapters for chicken here because I think that chicken thighs are so different in flavour from breast fillets. It's also handy to limit your ingredients when you're cooking al fresco, so have a go at some of the delicious barbecue recipes.

# Beef

# Roast beef fillet with creamy Dauphinoise potatoes

This dish has to be the ultimate treat for a dinner party or special occasion. The wonderful thing about these Dauphinoise potatoes is that if you don't have two ovens they can be made in advance then reheated as individual portions on a baking sheet for about 20 minutes covered with foil at the same oven temperature as for the beef.

**1** 300ml (½ pint) cream
**2** 300ml (½ pint) milk
**3** 1 large garlic clove, peeled and finely grated
**4** 1.75kg (4lb) potatoes (e.g. Maris Piper or King Edward)
**5** 700g (1lb 9oz) thick end of a whole beef fillet (called the chateaubriand)
**&** sea salt and freshly ground black pepper; 1 tablespoon olive oil

**serves 4–8**

**step one** Preheat the oven to 150°C/300°F/gas 2. Put the cream and milk in a large jug with the garlic and season to taste. Peel and thinly slice the potatoes on a mandolin or using a food processor with an attachment blade.

**step two** Arrange a layer of the potatoes in a 2.75 litre (5¼ pint) ovenproof dish and spoon over a couple of tablespoons of the cream mixture. Continue layering in this way until all of the ingredients are used up. Press down the top lightly to ensure all of the potatoes are well coated in the cream mixture. Cover with foil and bake for 2 hours until the potatoes are completely tender. Remove the foil and bake for another 20–25 minutes until lightly golden on top.

**step three** Meanwhile, heat a separate oven to 200°C/400°F/gas 6. Allow the chateaubriand to come to room temperature before cooking. Rub all over with olive oil, then season generously. Heat a heavy-based ovenproof frying pan. Seal the chateaubriand over a high heat on all sides until golden brown; this should take about 6 minutes in total.

**step four** Transfer the frying pan to the oven and roast for 15 minutes per 450g (1lb) for medium-rare, or cook to your liking. Remove from the oven and allow to rest in a warm place for 10 minutes before carving into slices. Cut the Dauphinoise potatoes into portions and arrange on warmed plates with the slices of beef to serve.

# Rare roast beef and blue cheese salad

This is a great dish to make if you want very little left to do at the last minute as you can leave the covered beef to stand for up to two hours before slicing.

1. 500g (1lb 2oz) well-hung beef fillet, trimmed
2. 1 x 200g (7oz) bag mixed baby salad leaves
3. 200g (7oz) baby plum tomatoes, halved
4. 225g (8oz) blue cheese, crumbled (e.g. Gorgonzola, Roquefort or Cashel Blue)
5. 1 teaspoon red wine vinegar
& sea salt and freshly ground black pepper; 4 tablespoons extra-virgin olive oil

**serves 4**

**step one** Preheat the oven to 220°C/425°F/gas 7. Heat an ovenproof frying pan until very hot. Season the beef. Add half the olive oil to the pan, pop in the beef and brown well on all sides. Remove from the heat, drain off any excess oil and then place the beef in the oven for 5 minutes. Remove from the oven and leave to stand in a warm place until the beef has relaxed. This will take at least 20 minutes.

**step two** When the beef has rested and you are ready to serve, place the fillet on a carving board and, using a sharp carving knife, cut into very thin slices. Arrange the salad leaves in wide-rimmed bowls, then fold the slices of beef into cone shapes and pile them on top of the salad leaves. Scatter over the baby plum tomatoes followed by the crumbled blue cheese.

**step three** Mix the red wine vinegar with the remaining olive oil, then season to taste. Add a good drizzle of the dressing over each salad to serve.

# Pan-fried beef fillet steak in green peppercorn sauce

The first thing to do when frying a steak is to ensure your frying pan is really hot. This will allow the steak to seal and start to fry as soon as it hits the pan, otherwise it will poach and you will lose the wonderful caramelization that should end up in the pan, which in this case is the basis for your sauce.

1. 4 x 175g (6oz) beef fillet steaks
2. 25g (1oz) butter
3. 2 teaspoons green peppercorns in brine, drained
4. 2 teaspoons Dijon mustard
5. 200ml (7fl oz) double cream
&. sea salt and freshly ground black pepper; 1 tablespoon olive oil

serves 4

**step one** Heat a heavy-based frying pan until really hot. Add the olive oil and then add the steaks. Cook for a couple of minutes on each side (a bit longer if you don't like your meat so rare). Remove from the heat and leave to rest in a warm place for a few minutes while you make the sauce.

**step two** Pour off the oil or tilt the pan and remove the pool of fat with kitchen paper, but do not remove the crispy bits. Quickly return to the heat, add the butter and when it froths add the green peppercorns, squashing some of them into the butter using the back of a wooden spoon.

**step three** Whisk in the mustard and cream then simmer for 2–3 minutes, whisking occasionally, until the sauce has slightly reduced and has a good consistency. Season to taste.

**step four** Arrange the pan-fried steaks on warmed plates and spoon over the green peppercorn sauce to serve.

# Seared beef with black bean sauce and purple sprouting broccoli

Although sirloin steak can be expensive the flavour and texture is well worth the extra money. If you don't fancy purple sprouting broccoli try using the long-stemmed variety or asparagus spears also work really well. I like to eat this with quick-cook noodles.

**①** 450g (1lb) sirloin steak, trimmed
**②** 450g (1lb) purple sprouting broccoli
**③** 4 spring onions, trimmed and thinly sliced
**④** 2 tablespoons freshly grated root ginger
**⑤** 1 x 125g (4½oz) sachet stir-fry black bean sauce
**&** salt and freshly ground black pepper; 2 tablespoons sunflower oil

**serves 4**

**step one** Cut the sirloin first into 1cm (½ inch) slices then into thin strips. Season generously with pepper.

**step two** Heat a wok over a high heat until smoking hot and then add half of the oil and swirl up the sides. Add the beef strips and stir-fry for 2–3 minutes until just tender and lightly golden. Tip onto a plate.

**step three** Add the rest of the oil to the wok and then add the broccoli and stir-fry for 1 minute. Sprinkle over 1 tablespoon water and continue to stir-fry for another minute until the water has evaporated.

**step four** Stir the spring onions and ginger into the broccoli and continue to stir-fry for 1 minute. Pour in the black bean sauce and allow it to just warm through. Stir in the beef and once it is heated through, season to taste. Share among warmed bowls and serve at once.

# Thai red beef curry with coconut milk

I find Thai food much lighter than Indian food, and more subtle than Chinese food. You can always add more or less curry paste, depending on how hot you like your curry. Here I've used rib steak, which is a very good value cut but needs long, slow cooking. If you want to reduce the cooking time, simply use a more expensive cut of meat, such as sirloin or striploin, and simmer for 8–10 minutes.

**1** 1 bunch fresh coriander (roots intact)
**2** 2 tablespoons Thai red curry paste
**3** 1 x 400g (14oz) can coconut milk
**4** 500g (1lb 2oz) beef rib steak, trimmed and cut into bite-sized pieces
**5** 350g (12oz) Thai fragrant rice
**&** salt and freshly ground black pepper

**serves 4**

**step one** Strip the leaves from the bunch of coriander and set aside a handful for garnishing, then roughly chop the remainder with the roots and stalks. Place in a mini food processor with the curry paste and 4 tablespoons of the coconut milk. Blitz to a purée.

**step two** Heat a wok with a lid until smoking hot and then add the curry paste and cook for 1 minute, stirring. Add the steak and stir-fry for 8–10 minutes until the beef is well sealed and the curry paste has slightly reduced.

**step three** Stir the rest of the coconut milk into the beef mixture and bring to a simmering boil, then reduce the heat, cover and simmer gently for about 1 hour, stirring occasionally, until the sauce has slightly reduced and the beef is meltingly tender.

**step four** After 40 minutes or so, wash the rice briefly under cold running water and place in a pan with a tight-fitting lid. Pour in enough water to come 2.5cm (1 inch) above the rice. Add ½ teaspoon salt and then quickly bring to the boil. Stir once, cover with a tight-fitting lid, reduce the heat to low and cook for 15–20 minutes until just tender.

**step five** Remove the beef from the heat and season to taste. Ladle the Thai red beef curry into bowls and garnish with the reserved coriander leaves. Serve at once with separate bowls of the Thai fragrant rice.

# Pork

# Roasted porchetta with rosemary

This recipe is perfect to feed a crowd and the shoulder of pork is the best cut to use as it has just the right balance of meat and fat. Porchetta is tastiest served warm, not straight from the oven. If you are nervous about tying up the joint with string, take the stuffing down to your butchers and ask them to do it for you. But give it a go, you'll soon get the hang of it.

1. 2 fresh rosemary sprigs
2. 2.75kg (6lb) boneless shoulder of pork, rind ready scored (at room temperature for 2 hours)
3. 50g (2oz) freshly grated Parmesan
4. 4 garlic cloves, peeled and finely chopped
5. 4 tablespoons chopped fresh flat-leaf parsley
&. sea salt and freshly ground black pepper

**serves 6–8**

**step one** Preheat the oven to 190°C/375°F/gas 5. Strip the rosemary leaves from their stalks and finely chop. Cut the strings from the shoulder of pork and open it out onto a clean work surface, then season generously. Sprinkle over the chopped rosemary with the Parmesan, garlic and parsley. Tightly roll the pork back up to enclose the filling completely.

**step two** Tie with string at 2cm (¾ inch) intervals, working from both ends towards the centre; this keeps the meat in shape. Wipe off any excess moisture with kitchen paper and sprinkle with salt.

**step three** Place the pork in a roasting tin and roast for 20 minutes per 450g (1lb) plus 20 minutes. For the last 20 minutes of cooking time, increase the oven temperature to 220°C/425°F/gas 7. If your joint is exactly 2.75kg (6lb), it will take 2 hours and 20 minutes until cooked through and tender with crispy crackling.

**step four** Remove from the oven and leave the porchetta to rest in a warm place for 30 minutes, as it is actually best served warm. Carve into slices and arrange on warmed plates, then spoon over the pan juices to serve, if desired.

# Parma wrapped pork fillet with mozzarella and pesto

The crispy, salty flavour of Parma ham blends well with the natural sweetness of the pesto and enhances the succulence of the pork. Don't be too precious when stuffing the pork, just make sure that you enclose the filling completely.

**❶** 450g (1lb) tenderloin pork fillet
**❷** 2 tablespoons ready-made pesto (good quality)
**❸** 120g (4½oz) buffalo mozzarella, roughly chopped
**❹** 5 slices Parma ham
**❺** 675g (1½lb) spinach, washed, with tough stalks removed
**&** sea salt and freshly ground black pepper; 1 tablespoon extra-virgin olive oil

**serves 4**

**step one** Preheat the oven to 200°C/400°F/gas 6. Trim the pork fillet and split lengthways, without cutting right through. Open the fillet out flat and season generously with black pepper. I like to then cover it with clingfilm before gently bashing out the sides with the smooth end of a meat mallet or a rolling pin.

**step two** Spread the pesto over the pork fillet and then scatter the mozzarella down the middle and season lightly with salt. Arrange the slices of Parma ham in a slightly overlapping layer on the work surface. Then close up the pork fillet to enclose the filling completely and wrap with the Parma ham. Tie loosely with kitchen string at 2.5cm (1 inch) intervals and arrange in a roasting tin, seam-side down.

**step three** Cover with foil and bake for 15 minutes, then remove the foil and cook for another 25–30 minutes or until the pork is cooked through and the Parma ham crispy. Remove from the oven and leave to rest in a warm place for 5 minutes.

**step four** Meanwhile, prepare the spinach. Heat a large, heavy-based pan and add fistfuls of the washed spinach, adding another as one wilts down. Cook for 1 minute, then tip into a colander and gently press out all the excess moisture.

**step five** Heat the olive oil in the pan and then add the drained spinach. Season to taste. Toss until heated through. Carve the Parma-wrapped pork into slices and arrange on warmed plates with the wilted spinach. Spoon over the pan juices to serve.

# Baked bacon chops in cider sauce

A great way of cooking bacon chops in the oven. Look out for the ones that look like thick rashers, preferably dry cured. You could also buy a 750g (1¾lb) rindless loin of bacon and cut it yourself into four thick chops. These are delicious with my Buttered Savoy cabbage (page 146) and Celeriac and potato mash (page 151).

1. 4 x 175g (6oz) bacon chops
2. 1 tablespoon prepared English mustard
3. 25g (1oz) demerara sugar
4. 300ml (½ pint) dry cider
5. 2 tablespoons plain flour
&. freshly ground black pepper; 2 tablespoons olive oil

**serves 4**

**step one** Place the bacon chops, side by side, in an ovenproof dish that fits them snugly. Mix together the mustard and sugar in a small bowl with 2 tablespoons of the cider to make a smooth paste. Spread over the chops, cover with clingfilm and leave to marinate for at least 10 minutes, or up to 2 hours is great, turning once or twice.

**step two** Preheat the oven to 200°C/400°F/gas 6. Remove the clingfilm from the chops and bake for 15 minutes. Meanwhile, heat the oil in a pan, stir in the flour and cook for 1 minute, stirring. Gradually whisk in the remaining cider and cook for another 2–3 minutes until the sauce is smooth and thickened, whisking continuously. Season to taste with pepper.

**step three** Remove the chops from the oven and pour over the cider sauce. Bake for another 15 minutes until the chops are cooked through and tender. Transfer the bacon chops to warmed plates and spoon over the cider sauce to serve.

# Brine-roasted, apple-glazed pork chops

Let's really get cooking! After only one day in this homemade brine, these thick pork chops are seasoned all the way through, not just on the surface, and cooked to perfection they will be succulent beyond compare. The sugar in the brine also helps the chops brown beautifully, while the Bramley apple sauce adds a wonderful sticky glaze.

**❶** 50g (2oz) light muscovado sugar
**❷** 4 garlic cloves, peeled and halved
**❸** 4 centre-cut boneless loin pork chops, each about 2.5cm (1 inch) thick
**❹** 4 tablespoons Bramley apple sauce (from a jar)
**❺** 25g (1oz) unsalted butter, diced
**&** 100g (4oz) sea salt; 1½ teaspoons coarsely ground black pepper; 1 tablespoon sunflower oil

**serves 4**

**step one** To make the brine, place the salt, sugar, garlic and pepper in a pan with 1.2 litres (2 pints) of water. Place over a medium heat and bring just up to simmering point, stirring to dissolve all of the sugar and salt. Remove from the heat and transfer to a large non-metallic container large enough to hold both the brine and the pork chops. Leave the brine to cool completely, then chill in the fridge until completely cold.

**step two** Add the pork chops to the cold brine and make sure they are submerged. Cover with clingfilm and chill for 24 hours (no longer or the pork chops will become too salty). When ready to cook, remove the pork chops from the brine and pat dry with kitchen paper, then allow to come back to room temperature.

**step three** When the chops have reached room temperature, heat a heavy-based frying pan. Add the sunflower oil and then add the pork chops and cook for 10–12 minutes, turning once, until cooked through and tender. Spoon 1 tablespoon of apple sauce over each chop and dot the butter around the pan. Keep turning the chops over until they are nicely coated in the apple glaze. Remove from the heat and leave to rest for a couple of minutes before serving.

# Tomato risotto with crispy prosciutto

Prosciutto is the classic Italian ham that takes at least a year to mature, which allows a wonderful distinctive flavour to develop. If you have fresh basil leaves at home, fold a handful into the risotto just before serving.

**❶** 8 ripe plum tomatoes, peeled, seeded and chopped
**❷** 1.2 litres (2 pints) chicken stock
**❸** 350g (12oz) risotto rice (Carnaroli or Arborio)
**❹** 225g (8oz) Italian prosciutto, thinly sliced
**❺** 100ml (3½fl oz) double cream
**&** sea salt and freshly ground black pepper; 5 tablespoons olive oil

serves 4–6

**step one** Heat 2 tablespoons of the olive oil in a non-stick pan. Add the tomatoes, season generously and cook gently for 8–10 minutes, stirring occasionally, until you have a rich pulp. Remove from the heat and set aside.

**step two** Pour the chicken stock into a pan and bring to a gentle simmer. Heat a heavy-based pan, add 2 tablespoons of the olive oil and then the rice. Cook for 30 seconds to 1 minute, stirring until the oil has been absorbed and the rice grains have become translucent.

**step three** Add a ladleful of the simmering stock to the pan, stirring continuously until all the liquid has been absorbed. Continue adding ladlefuls of the stock, stirring all the time and making sure that the previous addition has been almost absorbed before adding the next. The whole process takes about 18–20 minutes, by which time the rice is tender but still al dente.

**step four** Meanwhile, heat the remaining oil in a large, non-stick frying pan. Add a few slices of the prosciutto and cook for a minute or so on each side until crisp. Transfer to a plate and repeat until all the prosciutto is cooked. Reserve 4 slices to garnish and roughly chop the remainder.

**step five** When the rice is just cooked, stir in the reserved tomato pulp with the cream and shredded crispy prosciutto, then season to taste. Share the risotto among warmed wide-rimmed bowls. Break the reserved pieces of prosciutto in half and use to garnish the risottos before serving.

# Lamb

# Roast waterfall leg of lamb with boulangère potatoes

This dish is hassle-free so perfect for a dinner party or Sunday lunch. The leg of lamb roasts on a rack directly over the layered up potatoes and onions so that they collect and absorb all the flavours and juices released from the meat as it cooks.

1. 3 onions, thinly sliced
2. 1.5kg (3½lb) potatoes (e.g. Desirée or Romano), peeled and thinly sliced
3. 300ml (½ pint) hot chicken stock
4. 1.75kg (4lb) leg of lamb
5. 2 garlic cloves, peeled and thinly sliced
&. sea salt and freshly ground black pepper; 1 tablespoon olive oil

**serves 4–6**

**step one** Preheat the oven to 220°C/425°F/gas 7. Heat the oil in a frying pan and sauté the onions for 3–4 minutes until softened but not coloured. Season to taste. Layer the potatoes and onions in a roasting tin large enough to sit neatly underneath the leg of lamb. Season each layer as you go and finish with an attractive overlapping layer of potatoes. Pour over the stock and set to one side.

**step two** Make small, deep incisions all over the surface of the lamb and insert the slices of garlic. Season generously.

**step three** Place the lamb on a rack set over the potatoes and onions and roast in the oven for 15 minutes, then reduce the temperature to 180°C/350°F/gas 4 and roast for 15 minutes per 450g (1lb) for medium-rare or 20 minutes for well done, plus 15 minutes. A joint this size should take about 1 hour and 15 minutes for medium-rare. Leave the lamb to rest for 15 minutes, then carve and serve on warmed plates with the boulangère potatoes.

# Pistachio nut crust rack of lamb

This is a twist on a traditional dish with a fantastic pistachio crust. Ask your butcher to French trim the racks of lamb for you. To do it yourself, remove the meat and fat from the rib bones leaving 4–5cm (1½–2 inches) of clean bones exposed.

**1** 50g (2oz) butter
**2** 50g (2oz) shelled pistachio nuts
**3** 50g (2oz) fresh white breadcrumbs
**4** 2 x 7-bone racks of lamb, each about 675g (1½lb)
**5** 2 teaspoons prepared English mustard
**&** sea salt and freshly ground black pepper

**serves 4–6**

**step one** Melt the butter in a small pan or in the microwave. Place in a food processor with the pistachio nuts and breadcrumbs and blitz until you have achieved fine crumbs. Season to taste.

**step two** Place the racks of lamb on a chopping board and, using a pastry brush, spread the mustard thickly over the fat side of each rack. Cover with the pistachio crust using your hands to press it down, moulding it over the lamb. Arrange the lamb, coated-side up on a baking sheet and chill for at least 30 minutes, or up to 2 hours is fine, to allow the crust to 'set'. Remove from the fridge 10 minutes before cooking.

**step three** Preheat the oven to 200°C/400°F/gas 6. Place the racks of lamb in a small roasting tin and roast for 20 minutes per 450g (1lb) plus 20 minutes for pink lamb, or longer if you prefer your meat more well done. Remove the lamb from the oven and set aside in a warm place to rest for 10–15 minutes, then carefully carve into chops and serve on warmed plates.

# Spitfire lamb with broad bean and pesto hash

This is a lovely recipe to make in the spring when lamb is at its best. Of course, you'll get great results with fresh broad beans but the frozen ones are always very good quality.

**1** 450g (1lb) baby new potatoes, scraped or scrubbed
**2** 4 x 175g (6oz) lamb loin chops or leg steaks, trimmed
**3** 225g (8oz) frozen broad beans
**4** 1 small onion, finely chopped
**5** 2 tablespoons ready-made pesto (good quality)
**&** sea salt and freshly ground black pepper; 1 tablespoon olive oil

serves 4

**step one** Preheat the grill. Halve the potatoes and place in a pan of boiling salted water. Cover and cook for 10–15 minutes or until tender.

**step two** Season the lamb chops or steaks. Place on the grill rack and cook for 5–6 minutes on each side until cooked through and tender. Remove from the heat and leave in a warm place for a few minutes to allow the meat to rest.

**step three** Meanwhile, drop the broad beans into a pan of boiling salted water and simmer for 3–4 minutes until tender. Drain and quickly refresh under cold running water to prevent them from cooking further. When cool enough to handle, slip the beans out of the grey skins. Set aside until needed.

**step four** Heat the olive oil in a frying pan and cook the onion for 2–3 minutes until softened but not coloured.

**step five** Drain the potatoes and mix into the sautéed onion along with the pesto and skinned broad beans. Check the seasoning and serve on warmed plates with the grilled lamb loin chops or leg steaks.

# Lamb steak heaven with orange and redcurrant jelly

Give these succulent beauties an extra couple of minutes on the griddle pan if you prefer your meat more well done. Of course they would also be heavenly delicious cooked on the barbecue or under the grill.

1. 1 orange
2. 1 tablespoon warmed redcurrant jelly, plus extra to serve
3. 1 teaspoon prepared English mustard
4. 1 teaspoon chopped fresh rosemary
5. 4 x 200g (7oz) boneless lamb leg steaks
&. sea salt and freshly ground black pepper; 2 tablespoons olive oil

**serves 4**

**step one** Finely grate the rind of the orange into a bowl and then squeeze in the juice. Whisk in the olive oil, warmed redcurrant jelly, mustard and rosemary. Season to taste and pour into a shallow non-metallic dish. Add the lamb leg steaks, turning to coat. Cover with clingfilm and set aside for at least 15 minutes, or up to 24 hours in the fridge is great, to allow the flavours to penetrate the meat.

**step two** When you are ready to cook, preheat a griddle pan until smoking hot. Shake off the excess marinade from the lamb and arrange the steaks in the griddle pan. Cook for 8–10 minutes until cooked through and tender, turning once. Press the lamb steaks down lightly with a fish slice if the meat begins to curl slightly. Remove from the heat and leave to rest for a couple of minutes. Arrange the lamb steaks on warmed plates and add a dollop of the redcurrant jelly to each plate to serve.

# Hallelujah! Harrisa-rubbed butterfly leg of lamb and roasted sweet potatoes

To butterfly the leg of lamb yourself, find the place where the long bone running down the length of the leg feels quite close to the surface. Split open the meat along that bone and carefully peel it back from either side. At the fatter end of the leg is a small group of smaller bones. Continue to cut the meat away from these bones until you have completely opened up the leg and can lift them out. Alternatively, ask your friendly butcher to do it for you.

1. 1 large garlic bulb
2. 2 tablespoons harissa paste
3. 6 tablespoons Greek strained yoghurt
4. 3kg (6½lb) leg of lamb, boned and well trimmed, roughly 5cm (2 inches) thick
5. 675g (1½lb) sweet potatoes (orange-fleshed if possible), peeled and cut into 2.5cm (1 inch) chunks
& sea salt and freshly ground black pepper; 4 tablespoons olive oil

**serves 4–6**

**step one** Preheat the oven to 190°C/375°F/gas 5. Cut off the top third of the garlic bulb so that the cloves can be squeezed out easily once cooked. Wrap tightly in foil and roast for 40–45 minutes or until the bulb feels soft when lightly squeezed. Remove from the oven and leave until cool enough to handle, and then squeeze the garlic pulp into a bowl. Add half the olive oil, the harissa paste and the yoghurt and mix to a smooth paste.

**step two** Place the lamb in a shallow non-metallic dish. Rub the harissa mixture all over the meat, then cover with clingfilm and chill overnight or leave to stand at room temperature for at least 2–3 hours.

**step three** Preheat the oven to 240°C/475°F/gas 9. If the lamb has been chilled overnight, bring it back to room temperature, then place, cut-side up, on a rack in a large roasting tin and season with salt. Place the lamb on the bottom shelf of the oven and roast for 15 minutes, then turn it over and roast for another 10 minutes for rare.

**step four** Meanwhile, toss the sweet potatoes in the remaining oil and season generously, then tip into a separate roasting tin. Place on the top shelf of the oven. The sweet potatoes will take about 18–20 minutes until cooked through and lightly charred. Toss them occasionally to ensure they cook evenly, then remove from the oven and keep warm.

**step five** Remove the lamb from the oven and transfer to a warm dish, then leave to rest in a warm place for 10 minutes. If you don't like your lamb too pink you can cover it with foil at this point and it will continue to cook as the juices relax. Carve into slices and arrange on plates with the roasted sweet potatoes to serve.

# Barbecue

# Maple-glazed pork spare ribs

It seems such a shame that supermarkets only tend to sell cut up ribs, so for a complete rack it's really worth making a trip to the butcher. I recommend you cook the ribs first in the oven to ensure that they are properly cooked through before finishing them on the barbecue.

**1** 2kg (4½lb) meaty pork spare ribs (in 2–3 racks)
**2** 150ml (¼ pint) maple syrup
**3** 1 teaspoon cayenne pepper
**4** 2 large garlic cloves, peeled and crushed
**5** 6 tablespoons tomato ketchup
**&** salt and freshly ground black pepper

**serves 4**

**step one** Preheat the oven to 190°C/375°F/gas 5. Arrange the ribs in a large roasting tin and roast for 45 minutes to 1 hour until just tender – this will depend on the size of the racks. The ribs can then be set aside at this stage until you are ready to finish them on the barbecue. If you aren't planning to cook them within a couple of hours, cover with clingfilm and chill, then bring back to room temperature before you use them.

**step two** Light the barbecue. Mix the maple syrup in a bowl with the cayenne pepper, garlic, tomato ketchup and seasoning. Brush all over the ribs and barbecue on medium-hot coals for 10–15 minutes, turning occasionally and brushing with more of the glaze, until the ribs are completely tender and caramelized.

**step three** Remove from the barbecue grill and give one last coating of the glaze so that they are nice and sticky, then cut between the bones into single ribs. Serve on warmed plates with plenty of napkins and finger bowls.

# Yakitori chicken skewers

These skewers are incredibly easy to make but taste so delicious they'll be gone before you know it. Traditional Japanese ingredients are now becoming much more widely available so look out for them in your local supermarket.

**①** 6 tablespoons Japanese soy sauce, plus extra for dipping
**②** 3 tablespoons mirin
**③** 2 tablespoons sake
**④** 1 tablespoon caster sugar
**⑤** 450g (1lb) boneless, skinless chicken thighs

**serves 4**

**step one** Put the soy sauce, mirin, sake and sugar into a small pan. Bring to the boil, then reduce the heat and simmer for about 5 minutes, stirring occasionally, until the mixture has reduced and become slightly syrupy. Place in a shallow non-metallic dish and leave to cool.

**step two** Cut the chicken thighs into 2cm (³/₄ inch) pieces and add to the cooled marinade. Cover with clingfilm and chill for at least 2 hours, or overnight is perfect.

**step three** Light the barbecue. Soak 8 x 15cm (6 inch) bamboo skewers in a shallow dish of cold water for 30 minutes to prevent them from burning on the barbecue.

**step four** Thread the chicken onto skewers and barbecue for 6–8 minutes on medium hot coals, turning and basting with the marinade now and then. Arrange on warmed plates to serve with small bowls of soy sauce to the side for dipping.

# Sticky hoisin sausages

These go down really well at the beginning of a barbecue and keep the hungry eaters satisfied before the main. Cooking them in the oven takes the pressure off space on the barbecue.

**①** 900g (2lb) cocktail pork sausages (good quality)
**②** 6 tablespoons hoisin sauce
**③** 1 tablespoon sweet chilli sauce
**④** 1 tablespoon dark soy sauce
**⑤** 2 tablespoons freshly grated root ginger

**serves 4–6**

**step one** Preheat the oven to 200°C/400°F/gas 6. Arrange the sausages in a single layer in a non-stick roasting tin.

**step two** Mix the hoisin sauce, sweet chilli sauce, soy sauce and ginger in a bowl and pour over the sausages, turning to coat.

**step three** Bake for 20 minutes, then drain off any excess fat, turn the sausages over and cook for another 10–15 minutes or until golden and sticky. Serve hot on a platter, skewered with cocktail sticks.

# Thai-style barbecued sea bass

Okay, so it's a fish, but it's such a good barbecue dish, I couldn't resist.

1. 4 x 350g (12oz) whole sea bass (or you could use snapper or grey mullet), cleaned and scaled
2. 4 tablespoons Thai red curry paste
3. 4 tablespoons coconut cream
4. 2 limes
5. 2 garlic cloves, peeled and thinly sliced

serves 4

**step one** Light the barbecue. Cut several deep slashes into both sides of each fish and place them in the centre of a square of foil.

**step two** Mix the red curry paste and coconut cream in a bowl to form a thick paste and rub it into the fish, making sure that some of it gets right down into the slashes.

**step three** Cut the limes into thin slices. Push one slice into every slash along one side of each fish, then sprinkle over the garlic. Fold over the foil to form a loose, well-sealed parcel and barbecue on hot coals for 15–20 minutes, turning occasionally, until the fish are completely cooked through and tender.

**step four** Place the parcels on warmed plates and allow each person to open their own, as the aroma is sensational. Garnish with fresh coriander if you fancy.

# Lamb kicking koftas

Serve these with lemon wedges, yoghurt and pitta warmed on the barbecue.

1. 1 onion, roughly chopped
2. 450g (1lb) lean minced lamb
3. 2 tablespoons harissa paste
4. 1 tablespoon ground cumin
5. 2 tablespoons chopped fresh coriander
&. salt and freshly ground black pepper; olive oil, for brushing

serves 4

**step one** Light the barbecue. Soak 8 x 15cm (6 inch) bamboo skewers in cold water for 30 minutes to prevent them from burning.

**step two** Blitz the onion to a purée in a food processor, then tip in the lamb, harissa, cumin and fresh coriander. Season generously with salt and pepper and blend briefly until the ingredients are just combined.

**step three** Divide the lamb mixture into eight pieces, then shape each piece into a long sausage around each soaked skewer.

**step four** Brush the koftas with a little oil and barbecue on medium-hot coals for 8–10 minutes, turning now and then, until lightly browned and cooked through. Arrange on warmed plates to serve.

# Chicken thighs

# Vietnamese-style sticky finger chicken

Chicken thighs are not only cheaper than breasts but they can be made much tastier. The secret of this recipe is in the slow cooking, which would leave a chicken breast dry and tasteless. When using thighs you end up with wonderfully succulent, well-flavoured meat. I like to serve these with some steamed fragrant rice and a bowl of stir-fried pak choy.

1. 4 tablespoons ketcap manis (Indonesian soy sauce)
2. 1 tablespoon freshly grated root ginger
3. 2 garlic cloves, peeled and crushed
4. ½ teaspoon Chinese five-spice powder
5. 8 boneless chicken thighs
&. 1 tablespoon sunflower oil

**serves 4**

**step one** To make the marinade, place the ketcap manis in a bowl with the ginger, garlic and Chinese five-spice, then mix well to combine. Arrange the chicken thighs in a shallow non-metallic dish and pour over the marinade, turning the thighs to coat well. Cover with clingfilm and chill for at least 2 hours, or up to 24 hours is best, turning the chicken thighs several times in the marinade. Bring back to room temperature before cooking and wipe off any excess marinade with kitchen paper.

**step two** Heat a frying pan over a medium heat. Add the oil to the pan, then place the chicken thighs in it, skin-side down. Reduce the heat to very low and cook for 20–30 minutes until the skin is nice and crispy. Don't be tempted to touch the chicken thighs while they are cooking or shake the pan, just leave them alone and you will produce the most fantastic crispy skin and succulent flesh.

**step three** When you can see that the chicken thighs are nicely browned and that the flesh is almost but not quite cooked through, turn them over and cook for another 5–6 minutes until completely cooked through and tender. Remove from the heat and leave to rest in a warm place for 5 minutes. Arrange on warmed plates to serve.

# Crispy chicken thighs with savoury Puy lentil ragout

I have always loved the combination of earthy lentils and crispy chicken thighs. Puy lentils are small and slaty-green and are available in 250g (9oz) precooked packets and cans as well as dried. If you can't find them I've used green or brown lentils with much success.

**1** 8 chicken thighs with bones
**2** 2 leeks, trimmed and finely diced
**3** 2 carrots, finely diced
**4** 2 celery sticks, trimmed and finely diced
**5** 225g (8oz) dried Puy lentils
**&** sea salt and freshly ground black pepper; 3 tablespoons olive oil

**serves 4**

**step one** Remove the bones from the chicken thighs and trim down the thigh meat. Place the bones and trimmings in a pan with half of the leeks, carrots and celery. Pour in 1.2 litres (2 pints) of water and bring to the boil, then reduce the heat and simmer for about 1 hour until you have achieved a well-flavoured stock. Strain the stock through a fine sieve and place in a jug. You will need about 300ml (½ pint) in total so you can reduce it down further after straining if you need to.

**step two** Heat a frying pan over a medium heat. Add 1 tablespoon of the oil to the pan and put the chicken thighs in, skin-side down. Reduce the heat to very low and cook for 20–25 minutes until the skin is nice and crispy. Don't touch the chicken thighs while they are cooking or shake the pan, just leave them alone and you will produce the most fantastic crispy skin and succulent flesh.

**step three** When you can see that the chicken thighs are nicely browned and the flesh is almost but not quite cooked through, turn them over and cook for another 5–6 minutes until completely cooked and tender. Remove from the heat and leave to rest in a warm place for 5 minutes.

**step four** While the chicken thighs are cooking, if using dried lentils, rinse in a sieve under cold running water, then place in a pan with 600ml (1 pint) of water. Add a pinch of salt, bring to the boil, then reduce the heat and simmer for 15–20 minutes or until al dente (just tender but still with a little bite). Drain in a sieve and set aside.

**step five** Meanwhile, heat the remaining oil in a pan and gently cook the rest of the leeks, carrots and celery for about 10 minutes until softened but not coloured. Stir in the cooked lentils and the stock. Season to taste and simmer for a few minutes until most of the stock has been absorbed and the vegetables are lovely and tender. Carve each chicken thigh into 2 or 3 slices. Spoon the savoury lentils onto warmed plates and arrange the slices of crispy chicken on top to serve.

# Tender chicken and butternut squash risotto

When you make this dish any leftovers can go to make delicious risotto cakes – crunchy on the outside, rich and creamy in the middle. Simply roll and flatten handfuls of cold risotto into patties. Coat in a mixture of breadcrumbs and freshly grated Parmesan, then fry them in butter until golden.

**1** 4 chicken thighs with bones
**2** 1 butternut squash, peeled, seeded and diced
**3** 2 large leeks, trimmed and finely chopped
**4** 1.2 litres (2 pints) chicken stock
**5** 350g (12oz) risotto rice (Carnaroli or Arborio)
**&** sea salt and freshly ground black pepper; 4 tablespoons olive oil

**serves 4–6**

**step one** Preheat the oven to 200°C/400°F/gas 6. Arrange the chicken thighs in a small roasting tin and season generously. Roast in the oven for about 40 minutes or until cooked through and tender. Remove from the oven and leave to cool, then cut the chicken into bite-sized pieces, discarding the skin and bones. Set aside on a plate.

**step two** Heat half of the oil in a large sauté pan, add the butternut squash and season. Cook over a fairly high heat for about 5 minutes, tossing occasionally, until lightly caramelized. Reduce the heat, add half of the leeks and cook over a gentle heat for another 2–3 minutes, stirring occasionally, until the butternut squash is completely tender when pierced with the tip of a sharp knife. Tip into a bowl and set aside until ready to use.

**step three** Pour the stock into a large pan and bring to a gentle simmer. Wipe out the pan used to cook the butternut squash mixture and return it to the heat. Add the remaining oil, then tip in the rest of the leeks and cook for a few minutes, stirring, until softened but not coloured.

**step four** Add the rice to the leek mixture and continue to cook for another minute, stirring to ensure that all the grains are well coated. Add a ladleful of the simmering stock to the pan, stirring continuously until all the liquid has been absorbed. Continue adding ladlefuls of the stock, stirring all the time and making sure that the previous addition has been almost absorbed before adding the next. The whole process takes about 18–20 minutes, by which time the rice is tender but still al dente.

**step five** Add the reserved chicken and the butternut squash mixture to the risotto pan and give it a quick vigorous mix to combine and heat through. Season to taste and ladle into wide-rimmed bowls. Serve immediately.

# Roast juicy chicken thighs with herb and onion stuffing

This could quite easily be a cheat's succulent roast chicken dinner. To complete the meal, parboil a couple of small potatoes per person and toss in a little oil and butter before tucking them around the stuffed chicken thighs to roast. Cook some frozen peas just before serving and you've got a great meal with very little effort.

1. 25g (1oz) butter, plus extra for greasing
2. 1 small onion, finely chopped
3. 50g (2oz) fresh white breadcrumbs
4. 1 tablespoon chopped fresh flat-leaf parsley
5. 8 boneless chicken thighs, well trimmed
& sea salt and freshly ground black pepper

serves 4

**step one** Preheat the oven to 180°C/350°F/ gas 4. Melt the butter in a pan and sauté the onion for 3–4 minutes until softened. Stir in the breadcrumbs and parsley, then season to taste. Divide the stuffing among the chicken thighs and then fold over to enclose, securing each one with cocktail sticks to prevent them from popping open when cooking.

**step two** Butter a small roasting tin and arrange the stuffed chicken thighs in it, then season the skins generously. Roast for 30–35 minutes, basting half way through the cooking time, or until the skin is crisp and golden and the thighs are cooked through and tender. Arrange the roast chicken thighs on warmed plates and serve at once.

# Chicken, leek and potato pot pie

This is real comfort food, which I like to serve with some buttered broccoli or peas. You can replace the chicken with bite-sized pieces of salmon, which just need to be sealed before folding them into the reduced cream sauce. Otherwise, try adding leftover cubes of cooked ham and/or roast chicken to the finished sauce.

**1** 6 skinless, boneless chicken thighs, cut into bite-sized pieces
**2** 2 leeks, trimmed and sliced
**3** 350g (12oz) potatoes (e.g. Maris Piper or King Edward), peeled and cut into bite-sized pieces
**4** 300ml (½ pint) double cream
**5** 1 x 375g (13oz) packet ready-rolled puff pastry, thawed if frozen
**&** sea salt and freshly ground black pepper; 2 tablespoons olive oil

**serves 4**

**step one** Preheat the oven to 220°C/425°F/gas 7. Season the chicken thigh pieces. Heat half the oil in a large heavy-based frying pan and add the chicken pieces, then fry over a moderate heat until just sealed. Remove from the pan with a slotted spoon and set aside on a plate.

**step two** Add the remaining oil to the frying pan, tip in the leeks and potatoes and fry over a moderate heat for 5 minutes or until the leeks are soft and the potatoes are nicely coated. Return the chicken to the pan and pour over the cream (reserving a tablespoon for brushing the top of the pie). Bring to the boil, then reduce the heat and simmer for 3–4 minutes until the cream has slightly reduced and thickened and the potatoes are almost tender. Season to taste.

**step three** Transfer the chicken and potato mixture to a 1.2 litre (2 pint) pie dish and allow to cool slightly. Meanwhile, roll out the ready-rolled pastry to a slightly larger round than the pie dish and cut out. Cut the trimmings into long thin strips about 2.5cm (1 inch) wide (but don't be too fussy). Dampen the rim of the pie dish with water and then line with the pastry strips. Brush with a little more water and then cover with the pastry lid. Press the edges firmly to seal, then trim the edges and flute with the back of a knife.

**step four** Brush the top with the reserved tablespoon of cream (but not the sides, as this will stop the pastry from rising). Bake for 25–30 minutes until the pastry is golden brown and the filling is piping hot. Serve straight to the table and allow people to help themselves.

# Chicken pieces

# Seared chicken with guacamole, tomato and lime

I like to cook this chicken on a ridged griddle pan as it gives the chicken lovely markings and a wonderful smoky taste but you can just as well use a non-stick frying pan. If time allows, leave the chicken to marinate in the lime mixture as it makes it incredibly tender. This chicken is also great stuffed into pitta pockets with some shredded lettuce.

**1** 1 lime
**2** 2 tablespoons chopped fresh coriander
**3** 4 x 100g (4oz) skinless chicken breast fillets, each cut into 6–7 slices
**4** 1 x 170g (5¾oz) ) tub of shop-bought guacamole (good quality)
**5** 1 plum tomato, seeded and diced
**&** sea salt and freshly ground black pepper; 2 tablespoons olive oil

serves 4

**step one** Heat a heavy-based ridged griddle pan or a large non-stick frying pan. Finely grate the rind from the lime and place in a bowl, then cut the lime in half and squeeze the juice from one half into the bowl. Cut the other half into four wedges and set aside.

**step two** Add the olive oil to the lime mixture with half of the coriander, a pinch of salt and plenty of freshly ground black pepper. Rub the mixture over the chicken slices, then cook on the griddle pan for 4–5 minutes until cooked through and golden brown, turning once.

**step three** Meanwhile, place the guacamole in a bowl and mix in the remaining coriander and the tomato. Season to taste.

**step four** Arrange the griddled chicken slices on plates with a good dollop of the guacamole on the side. Squeeze over the lime wedges to serve.

# Seared chicken fillets with honey, lemon and paprika

This is a sweet, sticky glaze, which will add extra flavour to your chicken.

**1** 4 teaspoons clear honey
**2** juice of 1 lemon
**3** 1 teaspoon ground paprika
**4** 4 x 100g (4oz) skinless chicken breast fillets
**5** 2 x 75g (3oz) packets mixed baby salad leaves
**&** sea salt and freshly ground black pepper; 5 tablespoons olive oil

**serves 4**

**step one** Place the two tablespoons of olive oil in a shallow non-metallic dish and add 1 tablespoon of the honey, half the lemon juice and the paprika. Season to taste and stir until well combined.

**step two** Cut each chicken breast in half horizontally and add to the honey mixture. Stir until well coated, then set aside for at least 10 minutes or up to 24 hours covered with clingfilm in the fridge if time allows.

**step three** Mix the remaining olive oil, honey and lemon juice, and season.

**step four** Heat a griddle or large non-stick frying pan until smoking hot. Add the chicken pieces and sear for 1–2 minutes on each side until cooked through and lightly caramelized.

**step five** Lightly coat the salad leaves with dressing, pile them onto plates and arrange the griddled chicken pieces on top to serve.

# Roast chicken breasts with spiced green chilli butter

For a milder flavour, replace the chilli with two crushed garlic cloves.

**1** 50g (2oz) butter, softened
**2** 2 tablespoons chopped fresh coriander, plus extra to garnish
**3** 1 mild green chilli, seeded and finely chopped
**4** 4 x 175g (6oz) part-boned chicken breasts (skin on)
**5** juice of ½ lemon
**&** sea salt and freshly ground black pepper

**serves 4**

**step one** Preheat the oven to 200°C/400°F/gas 6. Place the butter in a bowl and beat in the coriander and green chilli. Season.

**step two** Make three 5mm (¼ inch) slashes on each chicken breast. Place in a roasting tin, skin-side up. Press the spiced butter into the slashes and squeeze over the lemon juice.

**step three** Roast for 45–50 minutes or until completely tender and the skin is crisp and golden. Garnish with coriander to serve.

# Chicken and Gorgonzola pockets with roasted asparagus

Creamier blue cheeses such as Dolcelatte or Cashel Blue are best for this dish.

**1** 4 x 100g (4oz) skinless chicken breast fillets
**2** 100g (4oz) Gorgonzola, cut into 4 even-sized pieces
**3** 12 fresh sage leaves
**4** 8 slices Parma ham (or you could use rindless streaky bacon)
**5** 550g (1¼lb) asparagus spears, trimmed
**&** sea salt and freshly ground black pepper; 2 tablespoons olive oil

**serves 4**

**step one** Preheat the oven to 180°C/350°F/gas 4.

**step two** Starting at the thick side of each chicken fillet, cut a deep horizontal pocket into each breast. Stuff with a piece of the Gorgonzola. Lay three sage leaves on top of each breast. Wrap each one in 2 slices of Parma ham and tie with kitchen string or secure with a couple of cocktail sticks. Season.

**step three** Heat half the oil in a large ovenproof frying pan and fry the chicken for 1–2 minutes on each side until just sealed.

**step four** Meanwhile, toss the asparagus spears in the remaining oil. Scatter around the chicken parcels, transfer the frying pan to the oven and roast for 8–10 minutes until cooked through and tender. Remove string or cocktail sticks and arrange on warmed plates to serve.

# Sauté of chicken with tarragon cream sauce

Any combination of potato and vegetable will complement this dish.

**1** 50g (2oz) butter
**2** 4 x 100g (4oz) skinless chicken breast fillets
**3** 120ml (4fl oz) dry white wine
**4** 150ml (¼ pint) double cream
**5** 2 tablespoons chopped fresh tarragon
**&** sea salt and freshly ground black pepper; 1 tablespoon olive oil

**serves 4**

**step one** Heat the butter and oil in a sauté pan. Season the chicken breasts on both sides and cook for 1–2 minutes on each side until browned. Add the wine, allow to bubble down, then reduce for 3–4 minutes over a high heat, turning the breasts occasionally.

**step two** Add the cream and tarragon to the pan and season generously. Cook gently for another 3–4 minutes, basting the chicken breasts occasionally, until they are cooked through. Arrange the chicken on warmed plates and spoon over the sauce to serve.

# Fish and seafood

A few key additional flavours such as lemon or butter can really bring out the delicate flavours of fish and shellfish. Meatier fish can cope with punchier accompaniments such as chorizo or Cajun spices, and seafood goes wonderfully with chilli, but remember to keep it simple.

# Fish

# Crispy hake with black olives, chorizo and parsley dressing

Packed full of Mediterranean flavours, try this fantastic hake dish with a green salad and a nice bottle of crisp dry white wine. The key to its success lies in the quality of the ingredients so be sure you seek out the best that money can buy. This dish also works really well with cod or haddock.

❶ 4 x 175g (6oz) hake fillets, skin on and boned
❷ 100g (4oz) raw chorizo, skinned and cubed
❸ 100g (4oz) black olives, stones removed (good quality)
❹ 1 tablespoon chopped fresh flat-leaf parsley
❺ a good squeeze of lemon juice
& sea salt and freshly ground black pepper; 2 tablespoons olive oil

serves 4

**step one** Heat half the olive oil in a large heavy-based frying pan and add the hake fillets, skin-side down. Cook for 2–3 minutes until the skin is nicely crisp then turn the fillets over and cook for a further 3–4 minutes until cooked through and tender. This will depend on the thickness of the fillets. Transfer the cooked hake fillets to a warm plate and keep warm while you make the dressing.

**step two** Add the remaining olive oil to the frying pan and tip in the chorizo. Sauté for 2–3 minutes until sizzling and the chorizo has just begun to release its oil. Remove from the heat and add the olives, parsley and lemon juice. Swirl the pan around until the dressing is nicely combined and season to taste. Arrange the hake on warmed plates, skin-side up. Drizzle around the chorizo and black olive dressing to serve.

# Seared swordfish with mango and chilli salsa

Swordfish usually comes ready-cut into steaks. It is a dense, meaty fish, which works well with spicy flavours. Take care not to overcook it as it does dry out.

**1** 4 x 175g (6oz) thick swordfish steaks
**2** 1 small firm, ripe mango
**3** 1 small mild red chilli, seeded and finely chopped
**4** 1 tablespoon chopped fresh coriander
**5** juice of ½ lime
**&** sea salt and freshly ground black pepper; olive oil, for coating

**serves 4**

**step one** Heat a griddle pan until hot. Rub the swordfish all over with olive oil and season generously. Add the swordfish steaks to the pan and sear for 3–4 minutes on each side until just tender. The fish should be still soft and tender, if you press it.

**step two** Meanwhile, peel and dice the mango, discarding the stone. Place in a bowl with the chilli, coriander and the lime juice. Season and stir until well combined.

**step three** Arrange the swordfish steaks on plates with a good spoonful of the mango salsa and a handful of fresh rocket to serve, if liked.

# It's brill in tarragon and soured cream sauce

You can use turbot – or John Dory – equally successfully in this dish.

**1** 4 x 100–150g (4–5oz) brill fillets, skinned
**2** 2 small lemons
**3** 175ml (6fl oz) double cream
**4** 1 tablespoon chopped fresh tarragon
**5** 1 teaspoon sugar
**&** sea salt and freshly ground black pepper; olive oil, for greasing

**serves 4**

**step one** Preheat the oven to 200°C/400°F/gas 6. Grease a large dish with olive oil. Cut one of the lemons in half and squeeze out 2 tablespoons juice into a bowl. Stir in the cream with the tarragon and sugar. Season.

**step two** Arrange the brill fillets in the oiled dish and spoon over the soured cream sauce to cover completely. Place in the oven and cook for 10–15 minutes or until just cooked through and tender.

**step three** Transfer the fillets onto warmed plates and spoon around any remaining sauce. Cut the second lemon into wedges and add one to each plate to serve

# Griddled sardines with beetroot tzatziki

Only buy sardines when they are extremely fresh – stiff fresh, as they say in the trade. If unavailable, fresh mackerel or herrings are a good substitute.

1. 16 large fresh sardines or 24 medium, gutted and scaled
2. 1 x 350g (12oz) jar pickled baby beetroot, drained and finely chopped
3. 1 Granny Smith apple, peeled and cored
4. 200ml (7fl oz) Greek strained yoghurt
5. 1 tablespoon creamed horseradish
& sea salt and freshly ground black pepper

serves 4

**step one** Preheat a griddle pan until hot. Arrange the sardines on the griddle pan, lightly season and cook for 3–4 minutes on each side until cooked through and tender.

**step two** Meanwhile, place the chopped beetroot in a bowl, grate in the apple and mix in the Greek yoghurt and creamed horseradish. Season generously.

**step three** Share the beetroot tzatziki among plates and arrange the griddled sardines to the side to serve.

# Grilled plaice with red onion and caper butter

For a special occasion, substitute Dover sole for the plaice; otherwise small brill fillets or lemon sole would work well.

1. 100g (4oz) butter
2. 4 tablespoons finely chopped red onion
3. 1 lemon
4. 2 tablespoons rinsed capers
5. 4 large plaice fillets, each about 250–300g (9–10oz)
& sea salt and freshly ground black pepper

serves 4

**step one** Preheat the grill. Melt the butter in a small pan and tip in the onion. Cook and stir over a medium heat for 2–3 minutes until softened but not coloured. Finely grate a little of the lemon rind into the pan, then squeeze in about 1 tablespoon of the lemon juice. Add the capers and season to taste.

**step two** Arrange the plaice fillets on a non-stick baking sheet and spoon over enough of the butter sauce to just coat. Place directly under the grill for 4–5 minutes, without turning, until just cooked through and tender.

**step three** Warm through the remaining butter sauce. Carefully transfer the plaice fillets onto warmed plates. Spoon the butter sauce on top. Serve with lemon wedges.

# Salmon

# Buttery poached salmon on crushed new potatoes

Here I poach the salmon in a little emulsion made with stock, white wine and butter. It's really easy and imparts an amazing buttery flavour to the fish. I then use the poaching liquid to make a sauce that I crush with new potatoes, yum! If you have some chives in the fridge they make a welcome addition to the sauce.

1. 500g (1lb 2oz) baby new potatoes, ready-washed
2. 300ml (½ pint) fish stock or light chicken stock
3. 100ml (3½fl oz) dry white wine
4. 75g (3oz) butter, diced
5. 4 x 150g (5oz) salmon fillets, skinned and boned
&. salt and freshly ground white pepper

serves 4

**step one** Preheat the oven 180°C/350°F/gas 4. Place the new potatoes in a pan of boiling salted water, then cover and cook for 15–20 minutes or until completely tender. Drain well and keep warm.

**step two** Meanwhile, pour the fish or chicken stock into a sauté pan that will accommodate the salmon fillets comfortably. Add the wine and bring to the boil. Whisk in the butter over a medium heat and regulate the heat so that it is at a bare simmer. Season to taste and add the salmon fillets to the pan. Don't worry if the emulsion doesn't cover the fish, just turn the fish once during cooking. Poach for 6–8 minutes until the fish is just tender and still slightly pink in the middle. If you prefer your salmon more well done, then leave it a minute longer.

**step three** Remove the cooked salmon fillets with a fish slice and arrange on a warm plate. Season to taste, then cover with another plate or piece of foil to retain the heat – the fish will continue to cook a little here so be careful. Bring your cooking sauce to the boil and reduce by half as quickly as possible, whisking continuously. Season to taste and keep warm.

**step four** Lightly crush the cooked new potatoes with a fork and then add in about 75ml (3fl oz) of the sauce to just bind the potatoes but not make them sloppy, reserving the remainder. Season to taste. Share the crushed potatoes among warm plates, place the salmon on top and spoon over a little of the reserved sauce. Place the rest of the sauce in a sauce boat so that guests can help themselves.

# Simple succulent salmon fish pie

This fish pie doesn't actually need to be baked in the oven if you prepare it as soon as all the ingredients have been cooked: simply flash under the grill until heated through and the top is bubbling and lightly golden. Of course, you could jazz the pie up by adding herbs to the sauce and a couple of handfuls of prawns but this is the way kids tend to like it, nice and simple.

1. 675g (1½lb) floury potatoes (e.g. Maris Piper or King Edward), peeled and cut into chunks
2. 600ml (1 pint) milk
3. 550g (1¼lb) salmon fillet, skinned and boned
4. 75g (3oz) butter, plus extra for greasing
5. 40g (1½oz) plain flour
& salt and freshly ground black pepper

serves 4–6

**step one** Preheat the oven to 180°C/350°F/gas 4. Place the potatoes in a pan of boiling salted water, cover and simmer for 15–20 minutes or until tender.

**step two** Meanwhile, place the milk in a sauté pan. Add the salmon fillet, ensuring it is fully covered, then poach for 3–5 minutes or until just tender, depending on its thickness. Transfer to a plate with a fish slice and set aside until the fish is cool enough to handle. Flake into bite-sized chunks, checking for any stray bones. Strain the poaching liquid through a sieve into a jug.

**step three** Melt half the butter in a large non-stick pan. Stir in the flour and cook for 2 minutes, stirring continuously. Pour in the reserved poaching liquid, a little at a time, whisking continuously after each addition.

**step four** Once all the liquid has been added to the sauce, reduce the heat and simmer gently for 6–8 minutes, stirring occasionally, until the sauce has slightly reduced and thickened. Season to taste.

**step five** Drain the cooked potatoes and return to the pan for a couple of minutes to dry out, shaking the pan occasionally to prevent the potatoes sticking to the bottom. Mash the potatoes or pass through a sieve or a potato ricer if you like a really smooth finish. Beat in the remaining butter and season to taste.

**step six** Lightly butter a deep ovenproof pie dish and add a couple of tablespoons of the sauce. Scatter over the flaked salmon, then spoon the remaining sauce on top to cover completely. Allow a light skin to form, then carefully spread over the mashed potatoes to cover completely. Smooth over with a palette knife and fluff up with a fork. Bake for 25–30 minutes until the fish pie is completely heated through and bubbling at the edges and the potato is golden on top. Serve straight from the dish onto warmed plates at the table.

# Salmon fillet with a horseradish crust

This is a great dish for a dinner party as the salmon can be prepared well in advance ready to be cooked off at the last minute. If you really want to push the boat out, make up a sauce with a small carton of cream flavoured with a little mustard and some snipped fresh chives to serve on the side.

1. 1 egg yolk
2. 2 tablespoons creamed horseradish
3. 50g (2oz) fresh white breadcrumbs
4. 1 tablespoon chopped fresh flat-leaf parsley
5. 4 x 175g (6oz) salmon fillets, skinned and boned
& salt and freshly ground black pepper, 1 tablespoon olive oil

**serves 4**

**step one** Preheat the oven 180°C/350°F/gas 4. Mix the egg yolk with the creamed horseradish in a small bowl. Place the breadcrumbs in a shallow dish with the parsley and season generously. Brush the top of the salmon fillets with the horseradish mixture, and then dip into the breadcrumb mixture to coat completely.

**step two** Heat a heavy-based ovenproof frying pan until hot. Add the olive oil and then add the salmon, crust-side down, and cook for 3 minutes or until the breadcrumbs are beginning to crisp up nicely. Turn the salmon over and transfer the frying pan to the oven. Roast for another 5 minutes until just cooked through and tender. Arrange on warmed plates to serve.

# Roasted Thai-7-spice salmon with pak choy and lime

This is a very simple recipe and one of my favourite ways of cooking pak choy. This technique also works well with Chinese cabbage or any other leafy green vegetable for that matter. To give it a bit of a kick, why not throw in a thinly sliced chilli or a sprinkling of chilli flakes.

1. 2 teaspoons Thai-7-spice seasoning
2. 4 x 150g (5oz) salmon fillets, skin on and scaled
3. 1 bunch spring onions, trimmed and thinly sliced
4. 400g (14oz) pak choy, cut across into 2.5cm (1 inch) wide strips
5. 1 lime, cut into quarters, pips removed
&. 2 tablespoons sunflower oil

serves 4

**step one** Preheat the oven to 180°C/350°F/gas 4. Place the Thai-7-spice seasoning on a flat plate and use to dust the salmon fillets, shaking off any excess. Heat an ovenproof frying pan or griddle pan. Add half the sunflower oil and sear the salmon, skin-side down, for 30 seconds, then turn over and cook for another minute. Transfer to the oven and roast for 6 minutes or until tender but still very moist in the middle.

**step two** Meanwhile, heat a wok until smoking hot. Add the remaining sunflower oil and swirl up the sides. Tip in the spring onions and chilli and stir-fry for 30 seconds or so.

**step three** Add the pak choy and stir-fry for another minute, then sprinkle over 1 tablespoon of water, reduce the heat and steam-fry for 1–2 minutes until just tender but still with a little crunch. Share among warmed plates. Remove the salmon from the oven and place on top of the pak choy. Garnish with the lime quarters to serve.

# Blackened Cajun salmon with lime aioli

Salmon is very reasonable these days, look out for wild Alaskan or organic varieties for the best flavour. I find it a very versatile fish and, because it's got a naturally high fat content, it's perfect for roasting or grilling.

**1** 2 teaspoons Cajun seasoning

**2** 4 x 150g (5oz) salmon fillets, skin on, scaled and boned

**3** 3 tablespoons mayonnaise

**4** 1 garlic clove, peeled and crushed

**5** 1 lime

**&** salt and freshly ground black pepper; 2 tablespoons extra-virgin olive oil

**serves 4**

**step one** Preheat the oven to 180°C/350°F/gas 4. Place the Cajun seasoning on a flat plate and use to dust the salmon fillets, shaking off any excess. Heat an ovenproof frying pan or griddle pan. Add half the olive oil and sear the salmon, skin-side down, for 30 seconds, then turn over and cook for 1 minute. Transfer to the oven and roast for 6 minutes or until tender but still very moist in the middle.

**step two** Put the mayonnaise in a bowl and beat in the remaining olive oil with the garlic. Add a light grating of lime zest and then cut the lime in half and add a squeeze of the juice from one half. Season to taste and mix well to combine.

**step three** Arrange the blackened Cajun salmon on plates and add 1 tablespoon of the lime aioli to the side of each one. Cut the remaining lime half into quarters and add a quarter to each plate to serve.

# Shellfish

# Langoustine risotto with a chilli kick

One of Italy's great simple dishes, perfect entertaining food and still very fashionable at the moment. This risotto is really for a very special occasion as it uses langoustines, otherwise known as Dublin Bay prawns or Norway lobsters. You could use tiger prawns but the flavour won't be as good.

1. 1kg (2¼lb) raw large whole langoustines (about 12 in total)
2. 2 large shallots, finely chopped
3. 200ml (7fl oz) dry white wine
4. 1 mild red chilli, seeded and finely chopped
5. 225g (8oz) risotto rice (Carnaroli or Arborio)
&. sea salt and freshly ground black pepper; 4 tablespoons extra-virgin olive oil

**serves 4 as a starter or double the quantities for a main course**

**step one** Break off the heads of the prawns and then peel the tails (reserving the shells) and remove the veins. Place the peeled prawns in a bowl, cover with clingfilm and chill until needed.

**step two** Heat 1 tablespoon of the olive oil in a pan and sauté half the shallots for 2–3 minutes until softened but not coloured. Tip in the prawn shells and continue to sauté for a few minutes until aromatic and then pour in half the wine, stirring while it bubbles down.

**step three** Add 1.2 litres (2 pints) of water to the mixture and bring to the boil, then lower the heat and simmer vigorously for 30 minutes until you have a well-flavoured stock. Strain through a fine sieve into a measuring jug, discarding the shells – you'll need 750ml (1¼ pints) in total. If you end up with extra, simply reduce down until you have the right amount. Put the stock in a clean pan and bring to a gentle simmer.

**step four** Heat 2 tablespoons of the oil in a sauté pan. Add the remaining shallot with half the chilli and cook for 2–3 minutes, stirring, until the shallot has softened but not coloured. Stir in the risotto rice and cook for a few minutes until nutty and perfumed. Add the remaining wine and allow to bubble away, stirring.

**step five** Add a ladleful of the simmering stock to the pan, stirring continuously until all the liquid has been absorbed. Continue adding ladlefuls of the stock, stirring all the time and making sure that the previous addition has been almost absorbed before adding the next. The whole process takes about 18–20 minutes, by which time the rice is tender but still al dente.

**step six** Heat the remaining oil in a wok. Add the rest of the chilli and stir-fry for 20 seconds. Tip in the peeled prawns and stir-fry for 1–2 minutes until just tender, then season to taste. Ladle the risotto into wide-rimmed bowls and arrange the sautéd chilli prawns on top to serve.

# Wok-fried clams with spring onions, chilli and ginger

This is a great way of cooking clams but you could also use mussels and just steam them for a minute longer. I like to use carpetshell clams.

**1** 1kg (2¼lb) fresh clams, cleaned
**2** 50g (2oz) butter
**3** 4 tablespoons sweet chilli sauce
**4** 5cm (2 inch) piece fresh root ginger, peeled and shredded
**5** 4 spring onions, finely chopped

**serves 4 as a starter or double the quantities for a main meal**

**step one** Rinse the clams in cold running water, discarding any with broken shells or that refuse to close when tapped sharply on the work surface. Place in a pan with a tight-fitting lid and steam for 2 minutes until opened. Shake the pan vigorously and discard any that have not opened.

**step two** Heat a wok or large frying pan until almost smoking. Add the butter, sweet chilli sauce, ginger and spring onions and stir together until the butter has melted, then simmer for 1 minute until bubbling.

**step three** Tip the steamed clams into the wok and toss a couple of times so that all the sauce coats the clams. Transfer to warmed bowls and serve with warm bread.

# Moules marinière

I like to serve this dish with French fries or crusty bread to mop up the delicious juices.

**1** 1 shallot, finely chopped
**2** 150ml (¼ pint) dry white wine
**3** 1.75kg (4lb) fresh mussels, cleaned (broken or open ones discarded)
**4** 120ml (4fl oz) double cream or crème fraîche
**5** 2 tablespoons of chopped fresh flat-leaf parsley,
**&** freshly ground black pepper; 2 tablespoons olive oil

**serves 4 as a starter or double the quantities for a main meal**

**step one** Heat the oil in a large pan with a lid, add the shallot and cook over a medium heat for 2–3 minutes until soft but not coloured.

**step two** Increase the heat, add the wine and mussels and cover. Cook for 2–3 minutes, shaking the pan occasionally, until the shells have opened; discard any that do not.

**step three** Using a large slotted spoon, share out the mussels among warmed large bowls. Whisk the cream or crème fraîche into the stock, bring to the boil and season with pepper, then pour over the mussels. Sprinkle with chopped parsley to serve.

# Pan-seared scallops with lemon butter

If your stock for this dish is too hot, your sauce will split; too cold and the fat will set. To test it, stick your finger in – it should feel warm, not hot.

1. 300ml (½ pint) chicken or vegetable stock (not from a cube)
2. 12 large prepared scallops (preferably in their shells)
3. ½ lemon, pips removed
4. 100g (4oz) unsalted butter, diced and chilled
5. 1 tablespoon snipped fresh chives
&. salt and freshly ground white pepper; sunflower oil, for frying

**serves 4 as a starter**

**step one** Pour the stock into a pan and reduce over a high heat to about 3 tablespoons.

**step two** Meanwhile, pat the scallops dry on kitchen paper. Heat a large frying pan, add a thin film of sunflower oil, then sear the scallops for 1 minute on each side until richly browned and crispy. Transfer them to a plate, squeeze over lemon juice and season.

**step three** When the stock has reduced, turn the heat down to its lowest setting and whisk in the butter, a few cubes at a time until it has melted and the sauce is light and frothy. Add a squeeze of lemon juice and chives. Season.

**step four** Arrange three scallops on each warmed plate, or back in their shells, and drizzle around the lemon butter sauce to serve.

# Calamari gets the nibble

This has to be one of my favourite nibbles, but it must be cooked to order.

1. 450g (1lb) medium-sized squid, cleaned (very fresh)
2. 2 tablespoons cornflour
3. 3 tablespoons semolina
4. 1 teaspoon ground paprika
5. 120ml (4fl oz) ready-made garlic mayonnaise (from a jar)
&. 1 teaspoon salt; vegetable oil for deep-frying

**serves 4–6 as a starter or tapas**

**step one** Preheat the oil in a deep-sided pan or deep-fat fryer to 190°C/375°F. Cut the body pouch of each squid open along one side and score the inner side with a diamond pattern. Then cut each pouch into 5cm (2 inch) pieces.

**step two** Toss the squid in the cornflour, semolina, paprika and salt to coat. Tip onto a tray, knocking off any excess. Leave for 1–2 minutes to allow the coating to dampen. This will give a crispier finish.

**step three** When the oil is sizzling hot, deep-fry the squid in batches for 1–2 minutes until the squid is tender and the coating is golden and crunchy. Drain well on kitchen paper.

**step four** Serve with the garlic mayonnaise.

# Side dishes

Green beans and cabbage can be dull on their own, but mix them with some herbs and spices and you have a delicious accompaniment. It's easy to forget about adding flavour to side dishes, but a well-balanced side dish can mean the difference between a good meal and a taste sensation.

# Vegetables

# Baked balsamic beetroot

This beetroot would also be wonderful served at room temperature as a salad with some orange segments, or alongside smoked mackerel with a dollop of horseradish cream.

❶ 6 large raw beetroot, trimmed
❷ 3 tablespoons balsamic vinegar
❸ 1 teaspoon cumin seeds
❹ sea salt and freshly ground black pepper; 2 tablespoons olive oil

serves 4–6

**step one** Preheat the oven to 200°C/400°F/gas 6. Peel the beetroot and cut each one into 8 wedges. Tip into a roasting tin, then drizzle over the vinegar. Sprinkle the cumin seeds on top and season generously, then drizzle over the olive oil. Toss well to combine.

**step two** Roast for 45–50 minutes, turning occasionally, until tender but retaining a bit of bite. Tip into a warmed bowl and serve at once or leave to cool and serve at room temperature.

# Braised peas with leeks

This is a clever way of jazzing up frozen peas or petits pois. We always have a bag in the freezer and I even find that they have more flavour than the fresh peas that you can buy these days (often out of season). Maybe it is because they are frozen within an hour or so of been picked whereas the 'fresh' peas have to get to us via a long supermarket chain.

❶ 50g (2oz) unsalted butter
❷ 2 small leeks, trimmed and finely chopped
❸ 450g (1lb) frozen garden peas and/or petits pois
❹ 4 tablespoons chicken stock
❺ a pinch of sugar
❻ salt and freshly ground black pepper

serves 4

**step one** Melt the butter in a large pan and gently sauté the leeks for 3–4 minutes until tender but not coloured.

**step two** Tip in the peas and/or petits pois and add the chicken stock and sugar. Season to taste, then cover and simmer gently for 4–5 minutes until the peas are completely tender and most of the liquid has evaporated. Check the seasoning, then tip into a warmed bowl and serve at once.

# Buttered Savoy cabbage with caraway

If you think you don't like cabbage, try this recipe, and you will be pleasantly surprised. It's just fantastic with Savoy cabbage but any green cabbage works really well with this technique. If you're feeling fiery, throw in a few chilli flakes when frying the caraway. It takes less than 5 minutes to cook, so start to prepare it just before you're ready to serve.

**1** 50g (2oz) butter
**2** a pinch of caraway seeds
**3** 1 Savoy cabbage, trimmed, core removed, and shredded
**&** salt and freshly ground black pepper

serves 4–6

**step one** Melt half the butter in a large heavy-based pan with a lid. Add the caraway seeds and stir-fry for 30 seconds or so until fragrant. Add 2 tablespoons of water and bring to the boil over a high heat.

**step two** When the emulsion is boiling, add the cabbage all at once with a pinch of salt, then cover the pan, shake vigorously and cook over a high heat for 1½ minutes. Give the pan another shake, cook for another 1½ minutes, then remove from the heat. Season with pepper, then tip into a warmed bowl and serve at once with the rest of the butter melting on top.

# Sautéd green beans with garlic and shallots

These beans would also be delicious with a couple of seeded and diced vine tomatoes added to the pan, but only in the summer when tomatoes are at their best.

**1** 275g (10oz) French green beans, tails removed
**2** 1 shallot, finely chopped
**3** 1 garlic clove, peeled and crushed
**4** 1 tablespoon chopped fresh flat-leaf parsley
**&** sea salt and freshly ground black pepper; 2 tablespoons extra-virgin olive oil

serves 4–6

**step one** Plunge the French beans into a large pan of boiling salted water, return it to the boil, then boil for a further 2 minutes until the beans are just tender. Drain, refresh under cold running water, then set aside.

**step two** Return the pan to the heat and add the olive oil. Tip in the shallot and garlic and sauté for 2–3 minutes until softened. Add the beans and continue to sauté for a minute or two until just heated through and completely tender. Sprinkle in the parsley and toss until well coated. Season to taste, then tip into a warmed bowl and serve at once.

# Honey-roasted carrots and parsnips

The natural sweetness of the carrots and parsnips is picked up by the honey, and the result makes the perfect accompaniment for my Roast waterfall leg of lamb with boulangère potatoes (page 93). The great thing about these veggies is that they are really very simple to prepare and take very little looking after.

1. 450g (1lb) carrots, peeled, trimmed and cut into chunks
2. 450g (1lb) parsnips, peeled, trimmed, quartered, cored and cut into chunks
3. 1 teaspoon chopped fresh thyme
4. 1 tablespoon clear honey
5. sea salt and freshly ground black pepper; 2 tablespoons olive oil

serves 4–6

**step one** Preheat the oven to 180°C/350°F/gas 4. Place the oil in a large roasting tin and add the carrots and parsnips. Sprinkle over the thyme and toss everything together until well coated. Season generously. Roast for 30–40 minutes until tender and just beginning to caramelize.

**step two** Drizzle the honey over the carrots and parsnips and toss until evenly coated. Roast for another 10 minutes or until the vegetables are just beginning to catch and the edges are caramelized. Tip into a warmed bowl and serve at once.

# Potatoes

# Crispy roast potatoes with garlic

The fat from roast meat makes the best roast potatoes. If you roast a goose or duck, save the fat and freeze it in ice cube trays, to use at your leisure.

1. 1.5kg (3lb) potatoes (e.g. King Edward or Desirée), peeled and cut into large pieces
2. about 6 tablespoons goose or duck fat
3. 6 garlic cloves, unpeeled
4. sea salt

**serves 4–6**

**step one** Preheat the oven to 220°C/425°F/gas 7. Place the potatoes in a pan of cold salted water and bring to the boil. Reduce the heat, cover and simmer for 8–10 minutes until the outsides have just softened. Drain and return to the pan for a minute or two to dry out.

**step two** Meanwhile, preheat a roasting tin with the duck or goose fat for a few minutes until just smoking. Put the lid on the potatoes and shake vigorously to break up and soften the edges, or roughly prod the outside of the potatoes with a fork. Carefully tip them into the roasting tin, basting the tops in the hot oil, and scatter around the garlic cloves.

**step three** Place the roasting tin back in the oven and cook for 40 minutes, then pour off the majority of the fat before turning the potatoes over. Season to taste with the salt and roast for a further 20 minutes until crispy around the edges and golden brown. Tip into a warmed bowl and serve at once.

# Celeriac and potato mash

This mash is fantastic served with fish, beef or game. It can be made a day in advance and reheated in the microwave or with a knob of butter on the hob.

1. 1 celeriac, top and bottom removed and cut into quarters
2. 550g (1¼lb) floury potatoes (e.g. King Edward or Maris Piper), peeled and cut into 1cm (½ inch) chunks
3. 1.2 litres (2 pints) milk
4. 50g (2oz) butter
5. salt and freshly ground white pepper

**serves 4–6**

**step one** Use a small sharp knife to peel away the thick, knobbly skin from the celeriac. Cut into even-sized 1cm (½ inch) chunks and place in the pan with the potatoes. Pour over the milk, bring to the boil, then reduce the heat and simmer for 15–20 minutes or until the vegetables are completely tender.

**step two** Drain the cooked vegetables into a colander set over a bowl to catch the cooking liquid, then tip into a food processor with the butter and about 6 tablespoons of the cooking liquid. Whizz for a few minutes until you have a smooth puree. Season and transfer to a warmed bowl. Serve at once.

# Home-made potato gnocchi like momma used to make

This classic Italian dish is traditionally served with pesto and freshly grated Parmesan, although I also like it in a simple tomato sauce. Gnocchi have an unfair reputation for being tricky and difficult to get right. In fact, they are extremely easy to make and a great way to get the kids involved.

**1** 900g (2lb) even-sized floury potatoes (e.g. Maris Piper or King Edward), scrubbed
**2** 175g (6oz) butter, plus extra for greasing
**3** 1 egg, lightly beaten
**4** about 200g (7oz) plain flour
**5** a good handful of fresh sage leaves
**&** sea salt and freshly ground black pepper

**serves 4**

**step one** Place the potatoes in a steamer and sprinkle with salt, then steam for about 20 minutes or until tender. Leave until cool enough to handle and then peel.

**step two** While the potatoes are still warm, pass them through a sieve or potato ricer into a large bowl. Add ½ teaspoon salt, 50g (2oz) of the butter, the egg and 150g (5oz) of the flour. Mix well to bind together.

**step three** Turn out the mixture onto a floured surface and knead gently, gradually adding more flour, until the dough is soft and smooth, but slightly sticky.

**step four** With floured hands, roll the dough into long sausages about 2.5cm (1 inch) thick. Cut into 1cm (½ inch) pieces, then roll each piece over the end of the prongs of a fork to mark grooves. Spread out on a lightly floured tea towel to prevent them from sticking together.

**step five** Bring a large pan of salted water to the boil and then lower the heat until barely simmering. Drop in the gnocchi, a few at a time, and cook gently for 3–4 minutes or until they float to the surface and are cooked through and tender.

**step six** Remove with a slotted spoon to a buttered serving dish. Cover with foil and keep warm while cooking the remaining gnocchi.

**step seven** When all of the gnocchi are cooked, heat the remaining butter in a frying pan and gently sauté the sage leaves for 30 seconds to 1 minute. Remove the sage leaves and set aside, then drizzle the butter all over the gnocchi, tossing to coat. Garnish with the sage leaves, sea salt and give a good grinding of black pepper to serve.

# Pan haggerty

Choose firm-fleshed potatoes for this recipe, which keep their shape during cooking and don't break up. This could also be baked in the oven if you prefer.

❶ 675g (1½lb) potatoes (e.g. Desirée, Romano or Maris Piper)
❷ a knob of butter
❸ 2 onions, thinly sliced
❹ 100g (4oz) vintage Cheddar cheese, grated
❺ salt and freshly ground white pepper; 1 tablespoon olive oil

**serves 4**

**step one** Peel the potatoes and slice thinly on a mandolin or with a very sharp knife.

**step two** Heat the butter and oil in a heavy-based frying pan that is about 20cm (8 inches) in diameter and about 5cm (2 inches) deep. Remove from the heat and cover the base with a layer of the potatoes.

**step three** Add a layer of onions over the potatoes and one of grated cheese, seasoning generously as you go. Continue these layers, finishing with a layer of potatoes and a sprinkling of cheese.

**step four** Cover the pan tightly with tin foil and cook over a very low heat for 45 minutes to 1 hour until the potatoes on top are just cooked through when pierced with a sharp knife.

**step five** Preheat the grill. Uncover the pan haggerty and place directly under the grill for 2–3 minutes to brown. Serve straight from the pan.

# Crushed new potatoes with basil and Parmesan

These potatoes are a kind of textured mash that you often see in trendy restaurants, so don't be tempted to make it too smooth.

❶ 675g (1½lb) baby new potatoes (e.g. Charlotte), scraped or scrubbed
❷ a handful of fresh basil leaves
❸ 6 tablespoons freshly grated Parmesan
❹ salt and freshly ground black pepper; 6 tablespoons extra-virgin olive oil

**serves 4–6**

**step one** Place the potatoes in a large pan of boiling water and return to the boil. Cover and simmer for 15–20 minutes or until tender, then drain well.

**step two** Tip the cooked potatoes into a large bowl. Add the olive oil and use the back of a fork to gently crush each potato until it just splits. Season, and then mix carefully until all the oil has been absorbed. Finely chop the basil and stir through the potatoes with the Parmesan, then season to taste. Tip into a warmed bowl and serve at once.

# Puddings and baking

I love puddings but they can often be complicated recipes. So here are a few of my favourite easy recipes – a lot less of the fuss and just as much of the 'wow' factor. There are tempting hot and cold desserts, scrumptious fruity puds, baking ideas for tea time and some very tasty breads.

# Cold classic desserts

# Chocolate and hazelnut torte

This keeps very well in the fridge. Try it with raspberries or crème fraîche.

1. 175g (6oz) unsalted butter, plus extra for greasing
2. 175g (6oz) roasted skinned hazelnuts
3. 175g (6oz) plain chocolate (70% cocoa solids), broken into pieces
4. 175g (6oz) golden caster sugar
5. 6 eggs, separated

serves 6–8

**step one** Preheat the oven to 180°C/350°F/gas 4. Grease a 23cm (9 inch) spring-form cake tin with sides no deeper than 7.5cm (3 inches). Line the base with baking parchment.

**step two** Blend the hazelnuts in a food processor for 30 seconds until finely ground.

**step three** Melt the chocolate in a heatproof bowl set over, but not touching, a pan of simmering water, then leave to cool. Beat together half the sugar and the butter until pale and creamy. Beat in the egg yolks and the cooled melted chocolate.

**step four** Whisk the egg whites in a separate bowl until they stand in soft peaks, then whisk in the remaining sugar until the meringue is stiff. Gently fold in first the ground hazelnuts, then the chocolate mix.

**step five** Spoon into the tin and bake for 40–45 minutes or until a skewer pushed into the centre of the cake comes out clean. Remove from the oven and leave to cool in the tin. Cut into slices and arrange on plates to serve.

# Panna cotta terrine

Panna cotta, from Piedmont in northern Italy, translates as 'cooked cream'.

1. 3 gelatine leaves
2. 100ml (3½fl oz) milk
3. 500ml (18fl oz) double cream
4. 100g (4oz) golden caster sugar
5. 1 vanilla pod, split and seeds scraped out

serves 6–8

**step one** Put the gelatine in a bowl and cover with cold water. Soak for 5 minutes until soft.

**step two** Pour the milk into a pan and warm to just below simmering point. Remove from the heat. Drain the gelatine and add to the milk, stirring to dissolve.

**step three** Pour the cream into another pan, add the sugar and vanilla pod and seeds and bring to the boil over a low heat, stirring constantly. Remove from the heat, stir in the milk mixture and remove the vanilla pod.

**step four** Rinse out a 900g (2lb) loaf tin with ice-cold water, shaking out any excess. Fill with the cream mixture. Chill for at least 2–3 hours or overnight until completely set. Turn out onto a plate, and slice to serve.

# Meringue basket with lemon curd cream and strawberries

This meringue basket can look extremely impressive and the light, crisp texture of the meringues is the perfect foil for the creamy filling and strawberries. This type of meringue has a smooth texture and wonderful gloss. It also holds its shape very well.

**1** 4 egg whites, at room temperature
**2** 225g (8oz) icing sugar, sifted, plus extra to decorate
**3** 150ml (¼ pint) whipping cream
**4** 150g (5oz) lemon curd (from a jar)
**5** 450g (1lb) strawberries, hulled

**serves 4–6**

**step one** Preheat the oven to 100°C/200°F/gas low. Line three baking sheets with non-stick parchment paper and draw a 19cm (7½ inch) circle on each one.

**step two** Whisk three of the egg whites with 175g (6oz) of the icing sugar in a large bowl set over a pan of simmering water, ensuring the bowl does not get too hot or the mixture will begin to crust around the edges. Whisk until the meringue stands in stiff peaks.

**step three** Using a piping bag fitted with a large star nozzle, pipe 2.5cm (1 inch) thick rings of meringue inside two of the circles. Make the base on the third circle, by piping from the centre and making a continuous coil of meringue out to the rim. Bake the meringues for 2½–3 hours until dry but not coloured.

**step four** When the meringues are nearly done, make another batch of meringue mixture with the remaining egg white and icing sugar. Remove the cooked meringue rings from the paper and layer up on the base to form a basket, piping a ring of fresh meringue between each ring. Return to the oven for another 1½–2 hours until the fresh meringue is crisp but not coloured.

**step five** Remove the meringue basket from the oven and leave to cool completely, then carefully peel off the parchment paper from the base.

**step six** To make the filling, lightly whip the cream in a bowl and fold in the lemon curd. Spoon into the meringue basket and then cover with a pile of strawberries. Give a good dusting of icing sugar to serve.

# Chocolate parfait terrine with fresh raspberries

Mmmm … milk or white chocolate can also be used for this rich mousse.

1. 450g (1lb) plain chocolate (70% cocoa solids), broken into squares
2. 4 egg yolks
3. 100g (4oz) golden caster sugar
4. 600ml (1 pint) double cream
5. 450g (1lb) fresh raspberries, to serve
&. grapeseed oil, for greasing

**serves 6–8**

**step one** Melt the chocolate in a heatproof bowl set over a pan of simmering water, making sure that the bowl does not touch the water. Remove the bowl from the pan and stir until completely smooth. Leave to cool.

**step two** Meanwhile, whisk the egg yolks and sugar in a separate bowl until light and fluffy. In a third bowl, whip the cream until it stands in soft peaks. Carefully stir the melted chocolate into the egg yolk mixture, then gently fold in the whipped cream.

**step three** Line a 900g (2lb) loaf tin with oiled clingfilm and pour in the mixture. Cover with clingfilm and freeze for at least 4 hours or preferably overnight until solid.

**step four** Remove the parfait from the freezer about 20 minutes before you are ready to serve. Turn out onto a flat plate and peel away the clingfilm. Dip your knife into a bowl of hot water and cut into slices. Arrange on plates and scatter around fresh raspberries and grated chocolate to serve.

# Zabaglione

Warm zabaglione is to die for. It can be used as a sauce on coffee or hazelnut ice cream or – with a change of liqueur – as a gratin of forest fruits. Use Grand Marnier instead of Marsala and pour the zabaglione over mixed berries arranged in a flameproof dish. Cook under a hot grill until golden brown.

1. 4 egg yolks
2. 4 tablespoons golden caster sugar
3. 120ml (4fl oz) Marsala
4. crisp biscuits, to serve

**serves 4–6**

**step one** Put the egg yolks and sugar in a large heatproof bowl and beat with an electric mixer until pale and fluffy, then beat in the Marsala, a little at a time.

**step two** Place the bowl over a pan of barely simmering water and cook over a low heat, whisking constantly, until the mixture starts to rise and is very thick and creamy.

**step three** Pour into glasses, and serve warm with crisp biscuits on the side.

# Hot classic desserts

# Tarte tatin

Tarte tatin is a caramelized apple tart that is baked upside down. The best way to arrange the apples in the tin is to start at the perimeter, in a pinwheel fashion, filling the middle after a full circle of halves is in place. Pack the apples quite tightly to prevent from falling over. The tarte can also be reheated in the oven for about 15 minutes if you'd prefer to serve it warm. Crème anglaise, anyone?

❶ 225g (8oz) ready-rolled puff pastry, thawed if frozen
❷ 1kg (2¼lb) crisp eating apples (e.g. Egremont Russet, Granny Smith or Cox) – you'll need 6 or 7 in total
❸ grated rind and juice of 1 lemon
❹ 100g (4oz) unsalted butter, at room temperature
❺ 175g (6oz) golden caster sugar

serves 4–6

**step one** Preheat the oven to 200°C/400°F/gas 6. Unroll the pastry onto a clean work surface and carefully cut into a round, 2.5cm (1 inch) larger than a 22–25cm (9–10 inch) heavy-based, ovenproof frying pan, tarte tatin mould or shallow cake tin (but not a loose-based one). Place the pastry round on a baking sheet lined with non-stick parchment paper and chill for at least 30 minutes.

**step two** Meanwhile, peel, core and quarter the apples and toss them in half of the lemon juice. Using a spatula, spread the butter evenly into the base of the frying pan, tarte tatin mould or cake tin. Sprinkle over the caster sugar in an even layer and then tightly pack the apple halves, cut-side up, in the base of the pan, forming a circle round the perimeter before filling in the centre. Cook over a high heat for about 15 minutes or until the apples are caramelized, cooked through and light golden brown, being careful that they don't catch on the bottom. Remove from the heat, then sprinkle the apples with the lemon rind and the remaining lemon juice. Leave to cool a little, if time allows.

**step three** Lay the chilled pastry sheet over the top of the apples, tucking in the edges, and turning them down inside the pan so that when the tarte is turned out, the edges will create a rim that will hold in the caramel and apple juices. Bake for 25–30 minutes until the pastry is golden brown and the apples are completely tender.

**step four** Leave the tarte in the tin for a minute or two, then loosen the edges with a round-bladed knife and invert onto a flat plate. Rearrange any apples that have become dislodged back into place with a palette knife and leave to cool, if time allows. This allows all the juices to be reabsorbed and the caramel to set slightly because of the pectin in the apples. Cut into slices and serve on slightly warmed plates.

# Jamaican sticky toffee pudding

An all-time favourite in our house, this pudding also works with Madeira or chocolate marble cake or even my Dead-easy banana bread (page 177).

❶ 2 x 275g (9½oz) Jamaican ginger cakes
❷ 50g (2oz) butter
❸ 100g (4oz) light muscovado sugar
❹ 120ml (4fl oz) pouring golden syrup
❺ 150ml (¼ pint) double cream, and extra for serving (optional)

**serves 4–6**

**step one** Preheat the oven to 180°C/350°F/gas 4. Cut each ginger cake into eight slices. Select an ovenproof dish that's big enough to accommodate all the slices and arrange them inside in a slightly overlapping layer.

**step two** Place the butter in a pan with the sugar and golden syrup. Bring to the boil, then reduce the heat and simmer for a minute or two, stirring occasionally, until the sugar has dissolved and a bubbling and lightly golden caramel has formed.

**step three** Stir the cream into the caramel and simmer for another few minutes, stirring occasionally, until you have a toffee sauce.

**step four** Pour the toffee sauce over the cake slices and bake in the oven for 15–20 minutes until bubbling. Serve straight to the table, with more cream if you like.

# Rhubarb sponge pudding

You can use thinly sliced Bramley apples for this pudding or, come winter, a bag of frozen mixed summer berries.

❶ 675g (1½lb) rhubarb, trimmed and cut into bite-sized pieces
❷ 275g (10oz) golden caster sugar
❸ 175g (6oz) butter, at room temperature
❹ 3 eggs, beaten
❺ 175g (6oz) self-raising flour

**serves 4–6**

**step one** Preheat the oven to 180°C/350°F/gas 4. Pile the rhubarb into an ovenproof 1.2 litre (2 pint) pie dish, with a slight mound in the middle, and sprinkle over 50–100g (2–4oz) of the sugar. The amount you need depends on the sweetness of the rhubarb, which will vary according to the time of year.

**step two** Meanwhile, place the remaining 175g (6oz) of sugar in a bowl with the butter and beat together until pale and fluffy. Add the beaten eggs, a little at a time, beating well after each addition. Fold in half the flour, using a metal spoon, then fold in the rest.

**step three** Spoon the sponge mixture over the rhubarb until the fruit is completely covered. Bake for about 40 minutes until the sponge is well risen, firm to the touch and golden brown. Serve straight to the table.

# Blackberry and elderflower crumble

Perfect to make in the autumn when blackberries are at their best. The elderflower cordial gives the dish a wonderful subtle fragrance. Serve it with some warm custard or a scoop of your favourite vanilla ice cream.

1. 450g (1lb) blackberries (or any other seasonal fruit)
2. 6 tablespoons elderflower cordial
3. 175g (6oz) plain flour
4. 75g (3oz) butter, diced
5. 3 tablespoons golden caster sugar

serves 4

**step one** Preheat the oven to 200°C/400°F/gas 6. Place the blackberries in a 1.2 litre (2 pint) ovenproof dish and sprinkle over the elderflower cordial.

**step two** Sift the flour into a bowl and rub in the butter until the mixture resembles fine breadcrumbs. Stir in the sugar. Sprinkle the crumble topping over the blackberries and bake for 25–30 minutes or until the crumble topping is golden brown and the blackberry juice is bubbling around the sides of the dish. Serve straight to the table and allow everyone to tuck in.

# Queen of puddings

This is a classic winner. It's great when you fancy something sweet but don't have much in the cupboard.

1. 4 eggs
2. 600ml (1 pint) milk
3. 100g (4oz) fresh white breadcrumbs
4. 4 tablespoons raspberry jam
5. 75g (3oz) golden caster sugar

serves 4

**step one** Separate three of the eggs into two bowls. Add the fourth egg to the egg yolks and beat together until well combined. Stir in the milk, followed by the breadcrumbs. Cover the egg whites with clingfilm and set aside.

**step two** Spread the raspberry jam on the base of a 1.2 litre (2 pint) pie dish. Pour over the milk mixture and then set aside for 30 minutes until the breadcrumbs swell up.

**step three** Preheat the oven to 150°C/300°F/gas 2. Bake the pudding in the oven for 1 hour until the custard is set and firm to the touch.

**step four** Whisk the egg whites until they stand in stiff peaks, then fold in the sugar to make a smooth meringue. Swirl the meringue on top of the cooked set pudding and return to the oven for 15–20 minutes or until the meringue is set and golden.

# Fruit desserts

# Melon and elderflower granita

This granita is half way between a drink and a sorbet – the mixture is so refreshing and the texture is icy enough to eat with a teaspoon. This one reminds me of sequins sparkling in a glass and it's a lovely course to serve after a spicy meal to refresh your palate or at a barbecue. It can also be made with great success in an ice-cream machine – simply follow the manufacturer's instructions.

1. 1 ripe melon (e.g. Cantaloupe)
2. 4 tablespoons elderflower cordial
3. 50g (2oz) caster sugar
4. juice of 1 lime
5. 600ml (1 pint) soda water or sparkling mineral water

serves 4–6

**step one** Cut the melon in half and use a teaspoon to remove the seeds. Scoop the flesh from the melon into a food processor and add the elderflower cordial, sugar and lime juice. Blend to a purée and then add the soda or sparkling water and blend again until smooth.

**step two** Transfer the mixture to a large plastic container and freeze for 2 hours until partially frozen.

**step three** Remove the partially frozen granita from the freezer and beat with a fork to break down all of the ice crystals, and then return to the freezer.

**step four** Continue to freeze the granita for another hour or so, removing it from the freezer every 20 minutes to beat gently and break down the ice crystals. The longer you leave it in the freezer the more icy the texture will become.

**step five** If you plan to make this more than a few hours ahead, then transfer the container to the fridge for 30 minutes before you are ready to serve and break up the crystals with a fork. Spoon the granita into pretty glasses and arrange on plates with long-stemmed spoons to serve.

# Baked pears with pecan nuts and golden syrup

This dessert is perfect for a cold winter's day – served with custard it really hits the spot. Honey instead of the golden syrup would be just as yummy.

❶ 50g (2oz) butter, plus extra for greasing
❷ 4 large ripe pears
❸ juice of ½ lemon
❹ 25g (1oz) pecan nuts, finely chopped
❺ 4 tablespoons golden syrup

serves 4

**step one** Preheat the oven to 200°C/400°F/gas 6 and grease an ovenproof dish large enough to accommodate the pears in a single layer.

**step two** Peel the pears, cut each one in half and use a teaspoon to scoop out the cores. Toss them in the lemon juice to prevent them from going brown and place them, cut-side up, in the dish.

**step three** Place the butter in a bowl and beat in the pecan nuts, then use the mixture to fill the cavities of the pear halves. Drizzle over the golden syrup and bake for 25–30 minutes or until the pears are softened and the sauce at the bottom of the dish is bubbling. Arrange the pear halves on plates and spoon over the sauce to serve.

# Marbled mango fool

As kids, we all adored mango fool and my late Mum would often make this for us. If the mangoes are ripe and sweet enough there should be no need for sugar, but you could always add a teaspoon or two of icing sugar if you need to sweeten the fool up.

❶ 2 ripe mangoes
❷ juice of 1 lime
❸ 150ml (¼ pint) double cream
❹ 6 tablespoons Greek strained yoghurt
❺ crisp biscuits, to serve

serves 4

**step one** Peel the mangoes and then cut the flesh into a food processor. Squeeze in the lime juice and blend to a smooth purée.

**step two** Place the cream in a bowl and whip until it stands in soft peaks, then fold in the Greek yoghurt. Finally fold in the mango purée until almost combined but still a little marbled.

**step three** Spoon the mixture into dessert glasses and chill for about 2 hours, then set on plates with crisp biscuits to serve.

# Iced berries with white chocolate sauce

Use any selection of frozen berries you fancy for this recipe. It looks amazing and very festive served in Martini glasses, but any pretty glass will do.

1. 350g (12oz) mixed frozen summer berries
2. 200g (7oz) good-quality white chocolate
3. 150ml (¼ pint) double cream
4. 3 tablespoons evaporated milk

serves 4

**step one** Pile the mixed berries into four pretty glasses set on plates and leave to thaw at room temperature for about 10 minutes. The idea is that the berries are iced but not frozen solid.

**step two** Meanwhile, break the white chocolate into pieces and place in a heatproof bowl with the double cream and evaporated milk. Set over a pan of simmering water and leave to melt, stirring occasionally, until you have achieved a smooth chocolate sauce.

**step three** Drizzle the warm white chocolate sauce over the iced berries and serve immediately.

# Pineapple carpaccio with chilli, mint and passion fruit syrup

This dessert is worth leaving at room temperature for a couple of hours before serving to allow the flavour of the syrup to penetrate the pineapple. Don't be tempted to add the mint to the syrup before it has cooled down, otherwise it will turn black and will not be as pretty.

1. 1 large ripe pineapple
2. 50g (2oz) caster sugar
3. 2 passion fruit
4. ½ small mild red chilli, seeded and finely shredded
5. 2 tablespoons finely shredded fresh mint leaves

serves 4–6

**step one** Slice the top and bottom off the pineapple, sit it upright on a board and slice away the skin and all the little brown 'eyes'. Using a very sharp knife, slice the pineapple as thinly as possible. Cover the base of a platter or individual plates with the slices.

**step two** Pour 120ml (4fl oz) water into a small, heavy-based pan. Add the sugar and bring to a gentle simmer, stirring until the sugar has dissolved. Remove from the heat. Cut the passion fruit in half and scoop out the seeds, and then stir into the sugar syrup along with the chilli and leave to cool.

**step three** When the syrup is completely cool, stir in the mint and drizzle it over the pineapple carpaccio. Cover with clingfilm and set aside at room temperature for 2 hours if time allows. Remove the clingfilm to serve.

# Tea time

# Jolly jam-in custard tarts

These are a favourite with all children – quick, easy and very moreish. Experiment with your favourite jam, such as raspberry or strawberry.

❶ 175g (6oz) plain flour, plus extra for dusting
❷ 75g (3oz) butter, diced and chilled
❸ 4 tablespoons apricot jam
❹ 120ml (4fl oz) ready-made custard (from a can or carton)
❺ icing sugar, to dust

**makes 12**

**step one** Sift the flour into a bowl and rub in the butter until the mixture resembles fine breadcrumbs. Stir in 2–3 tablespoons cold water until you have achieved a firm dough.

**step two** Turn out the dough onto a lightly floured surface and knead briefly, then wrap in clingfilm and chill for 1 hour, if time allows.

**step three** Preheat the oven to 200°C/400°F/ gas 6. Unwrap the dough and put back on a lightly floured surface, then roll out to a thickness of 3mm (¼ inch). Cut out 12 x 11cm (4½ inch) circles with a cutter or small saucer and use to line muffin tins.

**step four** Place 1 teaspoon of the jam in the base of each pastry case, and then top each one with 1 tablespoon of custard. Bake for 25–30 minutes until the pastry is cooked through and golden.

**step five** Remove the tarts from the oven and dust with icing sugar, then leave to cool for at least 15 minutes before serving on plates.

# Dead-easy banana bread

This is more of a cake than bread. The more over-ripe your bananas are, the better it will taste. It is delicious on its own but is also fantastic served in slices with a scoop of vanilla ice cream and drizzled with toffee sauce. For a delicious nutty experience add 50g (2oz) pecan nuts or walnuts to the mix.

❶ 4 ripe bananas
❷ 225g (8oz) self-raising flour
❸ 200g (7oz) golden caster sugar
❹ 100g (4oz) butter
❺ 2 eggs

**makes 1 loaf**

**step one** Preheat the oven to 150°C/300°F/ gas 2. Peel the bananas and roughly chop them up. Place them in a food processor and add the flour, sugar, butter and eggs. Blitz until the ingredients are evenly combined.

**step two** Spoon the mixture into a 900g (2lb) non-stick loaf tin and bake for 1¼ hours until risen and firm to the touch. Leave to rest for 15 minutes before turning out of the tin. Cut into slices and serve warm or cold.

# Tea-time griddled scones

Of course these scones can be baked at 220°C/425°F/gas 7 for 10–12 minutes until well risen and cooked through, but as their name implies, you can also cook them on a griddle. Here I've served them with butter and homemade jam, but of course they would be delicious with clotted cream…yum!

1. 225g (8oz) self-raising flour, plus extra for dusting
2. 100g (4oz) butter, plus extra for spreading
3. 50g (2oz) golden caster sugar
4. 1 egg, beaten
5. 2 tablespoons milk
&. a pinch of salt

makes 8

**step one** Sift the flour and salt into a bowl and then rub in 50g (2oz) of the butter until the mixture looks like fine breadcrumbs.

**step two** Stir the sugar into the flour mixture, then make a well in the centre and add the egg and the milk. Gradually mix together until you have achieved a soft dough.

**step three** Lightly dust the work surface with flour and turn out the dough. Roll out to a thickness of about 1cm (½ inch). Stamp out the scones with a 6cm (2½ inch) fluted pastry cutter. Gather up the trimmings and knead lightly into a ball, then roll out again and stamp out more scones until you have eight in total.

**step four** Heat a flat griddle or large frying pan over a medium heat. Melt a knob of butter and then add a batch of scones, the number will depend on the size of your pan. Cook for about 5 minutes on each side until cooked through and golden brown. Set aside on a wire rack to cool while you cook the remainder.

**step five** Split the cooked scones and spread with butter and a good dollop of jam if you wish, then arrange on plates to serve.

# Rocky road chocolate brownies

This is a great recipe to make with children for a special treat, as the results are pretty instant. They really are so delicious and would make a lovely present wrapped up in a nice box.

1. 4 x 60g (2¼oz) Mars bars
2. 4 tablespoons pouring golden syrup
3. 100g (4oz) butter
4. 50g (2oz) rice crispies
5. 100g (4oz) milk chocolate, broken into squares

**makes about 12**

**step one** Chop the Mars bars into small pieces and place in a pan with the golden syrup and 75g (3oz) of the butter. Cook over a low heat for 3–4 minutes until melted, then beat until smooth.

**step two** Fold the rice crispies into the Mars bar mixture until well combined. Transfer to a 15cm (6 inch) square shallow tin and spread out evenly with a spatula.

**step three** Melt the chocolate and the remaining butter in a heatproof bowl set over a pan of simmering water. Spread in an even layer over the brownies and set aside for at least 1 hour until set. Cut into bars and arrange on plates to serve.

# Lemon shortbread triangles

These rich shortbread triangles with a buttery flavour and sharp lemon tang have a meltingly short texture that's perfect with a cup of tea or hot chocolate.

1. 150g (5oz) plain white flour
2. 3 tablespoons rice flour
3. 50g (2oz) golden caster sugar, plus extra for dredging
4. finely grated rind of 1 lemon
5. 100g (4oz) butter, at room temperature

**makes 8 wedges**

**step one** Preheat the oven to 160°C/325°F/gas 3. Sift the flours into a bowl. Stir in the sugar and lemon rind, then rub in the butter with your fingertips – keep it in one piece and gradually work in the dry ingredients until evenly combined. Pack the mixture into a 18cm (7 inch) sandwich tin, then prick well with a fork and pinch up the edges with your finger and thumb.

**step two** Place the shortbread in the oven and cook for about 40 minutes until firm and pale golden. Remove from the oven and mark into eight triangles. Leave to cool for 5 minutes before transferring to a wire rack. When cool, dredge with sugar and cut into triangles. Arrange on plates to serve.

# Bread

# Schiacciata (Tuscan olive and rosemary bread)

Schiacciata, meaning 'crushed', 'flattened' or 'squashed' in Italian, is the name for a Tuscan flatbread. The dough for this savoury version is much like the pizza and focaccia made in other regions of Italy. Here I've studded it with olives but semi-sundried tomatoes or strips of roasted peppers would also work well.

1. 1 teaspoon fast-action yeast
2. 450g (1lb) strong plain white flour, plus extra for dusting
3. 1 fresh rosemary sprig
4. 300g (10oz) jar pitted black olives, drained
5. sea salt, for sprinkling; about 120ml (4fl oz) extra-virgin olive oil, plus a little extra

**serves 4–6**

**step one** Mix together the yeast and flour in a large bowl. Make a well in the centre and pour in 300ml (½ pint) of tepid water and 5 tablespoons of the olive oil. Mix well to achieve a soft dough.

**step two** Turn the dough out onto a lightly floured surface and knead for 10 minutes until smooth and elastic. Place in an oiled bowl, cover with oiled clingfilm and leave to rise in a warm place for about 1 hour or until doubled in size.

**step three** Turn the dough back out onto a lightly floured surface and knead for another 2–3 minutes, then roll out to a large rectangle that is about 1cm (½ inch) thick. Place on an oiled baking sheet and cover with oiled clingfilm. Leave to rise again for about 20 minutes.

**step four** Preheat the oven to 220°C/425°F/gas 7. Strip the leaves from the rosemary sprig. Prick the risen dough all over with a fork and stud with the olives, then sprinkle over the rosemary and salt. Drizzle with the remaining oil and bake for about 30 minutes until cooked through and golden brown. Transfer to a wire rack to cool and drizzle with olive oil to keep the crust softened. Cut into chunks to serve.

# Walnut and raisin bread

You really can't beat the smell or taste of homemade bread, it's the ultimate comfort food and preparing it is wonderfully satisfying. This loaf is delicious for breakfast and makes a lovely sandwich filled with creamy blue cheese and rocket. I find that it also toasts very well after a day or two.

**1** 550g (1¼lb) strong plain white flour, plus extra for dusting
**2** 50g (2oz) butter, plus extra for spreading
**3** 1 x 7g (¼oz) sachet fast-action dried yeast
**4** 100g (4oz) walnuts, roughly chopped
**5** 50g (2oz) raisins
**&** 1 teaspoon salt; sunflower oil, for greasing

**makes 2 loaves**

**step one** Sift the flour and salt into a large bowl. Rub in the butter until the mixture resembles fine breadcrumbs. Stir in the yeast, walnuts and raisins until evenly combined.

**step two** Make a well in the centre of the dry ingredients and then pour in 350ml (12fl oz) of tepid water. Quickly mix to a smooth dough, then turn out onto a lightly floured surface and knead for 10 minutes until smooth and elastic. Place in an oiled bowl, cover with oiled clingfilm and leave to rise in a warm place for about 1 hour or until doubled in size.

**step three** Divide the dough in half and then shape each piece into a roll. Put on non-stick baking sheets and cover each one with a damp tea towel. Leave to rise again in a warm place for about 30 minutes.

**step four** Preheat the oven to 220°C/425°F/gas 7. Remove the damp tea towel from the loaves and slash the tops with a sharp knife. Bake for 10 minutes, then lower the oven temperature to 190°C/375°F/gas 5 and bake for another 25–30 minutes until the loaves sound hollow when tapped on the bottom.

**step five** Transfer to a wire rack and leave to cool completely. To serve, place on a bread board and cut into slices at the table. Hand around with a separate pot of butter for spreading.

# Potato farls

Traditionally potato farls were a great way of using up a bowl of leftover mashed potatoes but made from scratch they're even more delicious. They can be served with a good old fry up or just some bacon and eggs for a light supper. Just be careful not to overhandle the dough or it will become tough.

**1** 550g (1½lb) floury potatoes (e.g. Maris Piper or King Edward), peeled and cut into chunks

**2** 50g (2oz) butter, plus a little extra for serving

**3** 175g (6oz) plain flour, plus extra for dusting

**&** ½ teaspoon salt; sunflower oil, for cooking

**serves 4**

**step one** Boil the potatoes in a pan of boiling salted water for 15–20 minutes until tender. Drain well, return to the pan and allow to dry out for a couple of minutes. Mash until smooth and beat in the butter with the salt.

**step two** Sift the flour into the mashed potatoes and quickly mix to a smooth dough. Turn out and knead very briefly on a lightly floured surface. Cut the dough in half and roll out until 5mm (¼ inch) thick, then cut into quarters. Repeat with the remaining dough.

**step three** Heat a flat griddle or large frying pan. Add a thin film of sunflower oil to the heated pan and cook a batch of the farls for 2–3 minutes on each side until slightly risen and golden brown. Repeat until all of the farls have been cooked. Rub a little butter on each one and arrange on a plate to serve.

# Clap-hand roti

Clap-hand roti are Caribbean flatbread that are traditionally served with a stew or curry. The idea behind the 'clapping' is to soften the bread and separate the layers. To serve, spoon some of your favourite curry down the centre of each roti, roll up and serve hot.

**❶** 225g (8oz) plain flour, plus extra for dusting
**❷** 1 teaspoon baking powder
**❸** 40g (1½oz) butter, diced and chilled
**&** 1 teaspoon salt; vegetable oil or ghee, for brushing

**serves 4**

**step one** Sift the flour, baking powder and salt into a bowl. Rub in the butter until the mixture resembles fine breadcrumbs. Make a well in the centre and stir in 6 tablespoons water to make a stiff but soft dough. Place in a bowl, cover with clingfilm and leave in a warm place for 30 minutes.

**step two** Turn out the dough onto a lightly floured surface and knead lightly until smooth, then form into four balls. Flatten slightly and roll out into 23cm (9 inch) rounds about 5mm (¼ inch) thick. Brush with the oil or ghee, fold in half, then into quarters, roll back into balls, and roll out again to the same size.

**step three** Heat a flat griddle or heavy-based frying pan over a medium heat. Brush each roti in turn with a little more oil or ghee, add it to the pan and cook for 3–4 minutes, turning frequently and brushing the surface with oil or ghee each time you turn it.

**step four** Remove the roti from the pan, place in your palm and quickly clap your hands together 3–4 times, taking care not to burn yourself. Wrap the roti in a clean tea towel and keep warm while you cook the rest. Serve warm with your favourite curry.

# Irish soda bread

This is a really quick bread that uses bicarbonate of soda, not yeast, as the raising agent. It's divine simply spread with some good butter and a little homemade jam, or maybe a hunk of Irish cheese, say Cashel Blue. If you don't have any buttermilk in the house, sour ordinary milk with the juice of a lemon.

❶ 450g (1lb) plain wholemeal flour
❷ 100g (4oz) plain flour, plus extra for dusting
❸ 1 teaspoon bicarbonate of soda
❹ 50g (2oz) wheatgerm
❺ 450ml (¾ pint) buttermilk, plus a little extra if necessary
❻ 1 teaspoon salt

**makes
1 loaf**

**step one** Preheat the oven to 230°C/450°F/ gas 8. Sift the flours, bicarbonate of soda and salt into a bowl. Tip in the bran left in the sieve and stir in with the wheatgerm.

**step two** Make a well in the centre of the dry ingredients and add the buttermilk. Using a large spoon, mix gently and quickly until you have achieved a nice dropping consistency. Add a little bit more buttermilk if necessary until the dough binds together without being sloppy.

**step three** Knead the dough very lightly on a lightly floured surface and then shape into a large round. Place on a non-stick baking sheet and cut a deep cross in the top. Bake

for 15 minutes, then lower the temperature to 200°C/400°F/gas 6 and bake for another 20–25 minutes or until the loaf sounds hollow when tapped on the bottom.

**step four** Transfer the bread to a wire rack and leave to cool for about 20 minutes. Soda bread is best eaten while it is still warm. Simply cut into slices and serve.

# Index

# Acknowledgements

**I always enjoy writing my acknowledgements as it reminds me of all the good people I've worked with on the book. It's true to say that without them my task would have been near on impossible.**

So a big thank you and a massive hug to my friend and creative partner Orla Broderick – hope the kids are getting to see more of their mum? To my commissioning editor Muna Reyal for her support, encouragement and guidance through salt, pepper and oil. Also Caroline McArthur who was always so understanding and to the rest of the team at BBC Books. To food stylist Stephen Parkins-Knight, for his energy, enthusiasm, great music and attention to detail in the studio. To our butchers and fishmongers, especially Allan and Carl at Stephen's butchers, and Ross, Stephen's fishmonger for fabulous produce. To Caroline at The Hop Shop at Castle Farm for supplying the wheat heads. To my food photographer Dan Jones for his sensational photography – hope the new addition to the family is doing well. Colin Bell for his portrait photography (didn't he used to play for Man City?). To all the lovely people and pets at Smith & Gilmour, especially Alex Smith, Emma Smith and Katrin Smejkal for their beautiful design (still missing those mid-morning coffees). My agents, Jeremy Hicks, Sarah Dalkin and friends at JHA – you guys are the best. To my wife Clare, and our great kids Jimmy and Maddie for eating their way through the book. Also to young Joe and my old pet dog Oscar Poska.